Business Grammar, Style & Usage

Alicia Abell

Mat #40695709

Aspatore books may be purchased for educational, business, or sales promotional use. For information, please email AspatoreStore@thomson.com.

ISBN 1-58762-026-X

For corrections, updates, comments or any other inquiries please email AspatoreEditorial@thomson.com.

First Printing, 2003
10 9 8 7 6 5 4 3 2 1

Publisher of C-Level Business Intelligence
www.Aspatore.com

Aspatore Books is the largest and most exclusive publisher of C-Level executives (CEO, CFO, CTO, CMO, Partner) from the world's most respected companies. Aspatore annually publishes C-Level executives from over half the Global 500, top 250 professional services firms, law firms (MPs/Chairs), and other leading companies of all sizes. By focusing on publishing only C-Level executives, Aspatore provides professionals of all levels with proven business intelligence from industry insiders, rather than relying on the knowledge of unknown authors and analysts. Aspatore Books is committed to publishing a highly innovative line of business books, redefining and expanding the meaning of such books as indispensable resources for professionals of all levels. In addition to individual best-selling business titles, Aspatore Books publishes the following unique lines of business books: Inside the Minds, Business Bibles, Bigwig Briefs, C-Level Business Review (Quarterly), Book Binders, ExecRecs, and The C-Level Test, innovative resources for all professionals. Aspatore is a privately held company headquartered in Boston, Massachusetts, with employees around the world.

Business Grammar, Style, & Usage

Table of Contents

Introduction

Wielding his red editing pen, my former boss, President Bill Clinton, used to mutter, "Words, words, words," as he slashed away unnecessary fluff from the speeches we'd given to him. Clinton wanted to speak *to* Americans, not *over* them, and he believed quite strongly that filling his text with unnecessary rhetoric only alienated the audience. Clinton was spot on. One of my colleagues used to say he was more Hemingway than Faulkner. Clinton wanted workers on the factory floor to understand him as well as the academics at Harvard and the members of Congress in Washington.

To achieve that goal meant never sacrificing the content or quality of an argument, but just framing it in a way that would keep our audience engaged, no matter what their level in life. It also meant keeping the President's speeches organized, so that he offered a coherent argument, not a rambling lecture that would require a decoder ring to figure out.

It's the same as talking to a doctor who can describe your condition in layman's terms, versus the one who's had his head in the books for too long. There's a reason, in the end, Clinton is often described as one of the greatest communicators of the last century – a title shared with Ronald Reagan and Franklin D. Roosevelt. While Woodrow Wilson delivered powerful speeches, and his texts are worthy of bound volumes, no one ever accused him of being too cozy with the lower classes.

Speaking *to* people, not *over* them, isn't easy. In fact, I'd argue that boiling down ideas into "Clinton-speak" is even harder than using the high-brow "industry-speak." But it's a skill that's essential to great communication, no matter what your field of expertise. And it's an approach that's as applicable to a memorandum from the CEO to shareholders as it is to a speech at a board of directors meeting.

8

Think about it: How many meetings have you sat through where the speaker loses you less than five minutes into the discussion? Maybe his talk is filled with language so technical that you need a Ph.D. to figure it out. Or it's so disorganized that it looks like the floor of your college dorm room. Perhaps he doesn't even try to connect with his audience – no jokes, no stories, just numbers. Or maybe he leaves you wondering what in the world he wanted from you.

There's simply no reason anything you hear or read should ever lose your attention or – even worse – intimidate you. The last thing any communicator should do, at any level, is marginalize his audience. The most important thing is to have your audience buy in to you and your message; the more comfortable they feel, the more they'll be engaged with what you're saying. You've received the highest compliment when someone in the audience leaves your discussion feeling as though you were talking directly to him.

This skill isn't easy to acquire, but you can start on your way by following five simple steps:

1. **Organize your message.** Like a good lawyer, build your argument in a coherent manner; the more your audience can follow along, the more attention they'll pay. There's a simple saying in the speechwriting world: First tell your audience what you plan to tell them; then tell them; and then close by telling them what you just told them.

2. **Make it easy to follow.** Arrange your points in a way that encourages your audience to follow along. I usually organize my points numerically throughout the speech. (For example, "Today I'm going to discuss three reasons to buy this book. First, this book will help you ... Second ...") Also, don't fill your speech with two-dollar words you learned on the SAT. People shouldn't have to carry a dictionary to follow you. That's not to say, of course, that

you shouldn't use descriptive language to help get your point across.

3. **Make your best points first and last**. When you're making your argument, put your best point first and your second best point last. You always want to come out of the gate strong and leave your audience with a good impression.

4. **Encourage your audience to like you.** If you can, start with a joke or a good story, even if it's recounting something you heard on the *Tonight Show*. The more you give the impression you're a regular person, the more people will like you, relax, and actually listen to what you're saying.

5. **Keep it short**. Most television programs last only a half-hour because people just don't have the patience to sit through anything longer. Your speech should never run longer than 30 minutes or, if possible, 20.

These steps are doable – and many of their tenets apply to other types of documents, as this *Guide to Business Writing* shows you clearly and concisely. You can even follow the steps without spending thousands of dollars on a speech coach. Eat your heart out, Woodrow Wilson.

Josh Gottheimer
Cambridge, Massachusetts

Writing Well For Business

Some General Guidelines

Know why you're writing. Before you begin writing, know what you want to say – and why you want to say it. Are you explaining a situation or a problem? Are you trying to convince the reader of something? Are you recommending a course of action? One way to ensure you know why you're writing is to make an outline of your main points beforehand.

By always remembering your purpose in writing, you'll keep yourself from wandering off track. You'll also avoid confusing the reader. If you don't understand what you're trying to say, how can you expect the reader to?

Know your audience. Effective writing of all kinds is tailored to its audience. Who – and how many people – will be reading the document? How familiar are they with the subject matter? Make sure the answers to these questions fit with the tone and level of detail you include in your document.

Another key is knowing how long your reader or readers will have to read your memo, report, or email. This will help determine its length. One frequently used guideline is one double-spaced page per minute.

You also need to consider how much information to include to meet your readers' needs. Put yourself in their shoes: What are they looking for? What questions might they ask?

Present the most important points first. A business report is not a murder mystery; your reader shouldn't have to guess what the conclusion will be. Present the most important point(s) at the beginning of your document; then use the paragraphs and sections that follow to support your conclusion.

The same goes for paragraphs and sections within the document. At the beginning of each new paragraph or section, state the main point. Then present the explanation or supporting details, preferably in descending order of importance. This theory works for individual sentences, too: Placing the most important words at the beginning and end of a sentence heightens their emphasis.

Be clear and concise. The first key to being concise is eliminating unnecessary information. Stepping away from your document and coming back to it later can help you be more objective about what is and isn't needed to convey your message.

The second key is eliminating unnecessary words. Qualifiers such as *very, fairly,* and *quite* rarely add meaning. In fact, because they're so overused, they often have the opposite effect.

Many commonly used phrases include useless words. Some wordy phrases and their replacements are listed below:

Replace:	With:
along the lines of	like
a majority of	most
a majority of the time	usually
as a general rule	generally
as per	as, according to
as soon as	when
at your earliest convenience	soon or by *x* date

as you may or may not know	as you may know
at a later date	later
at all times	always
at this point in time	now
avail oneself of	use
by means of	by
can be in a position to	can
due to the fact that	because
during the time that	while
for the purpose of	for
free of charge	free
have a tendency to	tend to
inasmuch as	because
in accordance with	according to
in advance of	before
in all probability	probably
in connection with	about
in many instances	often
in order that, in order to	to
in reference to, in regard to	about
in spite of the fact that	although
in the amount of	for
in the event that	if
in the matter of	about
in the near future	soon
in this day and age	nowadays, now
in view of the fact that	because
make a recommendation that	recommend
of a confidential nature	confidential

on account of the fact that	because
on the grounds that	because
owing to the fact that	because
perform an analysis of	analyze
pertaining to	about
prior to	before
pursuant to	since
the question as to whether	whether
regarding the matter of	about
subsequent to	after, since
the writer, the undersigned	I, me
up to this writing	until now

Other phrases are redundant:

Replace:	**With:**
absolutely perfect	perfect
actual experience	experience
adding together	adding
advance planning	planning
and et cetera	et cetera
any and all	all
at about	about
basic essentials or basic fundamentals	basics, essentials, fundamentals
both together	together
cancel out	cancel
check into	check
close proximity	near

combine into one	combine
complete stop	stop
completely full	full
consensus of opinion	consensus
continue on	continue
cooperate together	cooperate
current status	status
customary practice	practice
desirable benefits	benefits
each and every	each or every
end result	result
enter into	enter
exactly equal	equal
final outcome	outcome
first and foremost	first
first priority	priority
free gift	gift
future projections	projections
goals and objectives	goals
group meeting	meeting
honest truth	truth
joined together	joined
new innovation	innovation
no doubt but	no doubt
one and the same	the same
outside of	outside
over with	over
past experience	experience
past history	history

personal opinion	opinion
point in time	time
range all the way from	range from
the reason is because	the reason is or because
reduce down	reduce
refer back to	refer to
repeat again	repeat
resume again	resume
small/large in size	small/large
totally empty	empty
this particular instance	this instance
3 a.m. in the morning; 3 p.m. in the afternoon	3 a.m., 3 p.m.
whether or not	whether
young in age	young

The third key to being clear and concise is using short sentences and paragraphs. Try to keep sentences to between 20 and 25 words. Or simply break up sentences that extend more than two lines. In general, no paragraph should include more than one or two ideas, and a paragraph of more than six sentences or 10 to 12 lines is almost always too long. When in doubt, split paragraphs in two at logical breaking points. The same goes for sentences.

You don't want your writing to sound stilted. Varying sentence length and structure can help prevent this. Read your writing out loud to make sure it sounds natural.

Use simple, specific language. Some people think using complex language makes them appear intelligent; in reality, it only obscures their point and makes them look pretentious. Effective writers use simple words such as *start* instead of *commence, help* instead of *assist,* and *end* rather than *terminate.*

Here are some unnecessarily large words and their replacements:

Replace:	With:
abbreviate	shorten
advise	tell
ascertain	find out
assist	help
commence	start
conceptualize	conceive
conjecture	guess
demonstrate	show
duplicate	copy
expedite	speed
facilitate	help
functionality	features, functions, capabilities
indicate	say, show
initiate	begin
nevertheless	but, even so
obtain	get
optimum	best
orientate	orient
receive	get
terminate	end, fire
utilize	use

Here are some phrases that were once commonplace, but now appear stiff and affected. Avoid or eliminate them:

beg to inform	in due course of time
in receipt of	it has been deemed necessary
it has been demonstrated that	it has been shown that
it is found that	it is recognized that
it is the intention of this writer to	it is worthy of note
it may be seen that	it must be remembered that
permit me to say	please be advised that
pursuant to	what is known as

Also avoid clichés such as:

back to square one	back to basics
ballpark figure	beyond the shadow of a doubt
first and foremost	hit the nail on the head
last but not least	state of the art
take the ball and run with it	under review

Finally, good writers also choose concrete words and specific examples over abstract, vague language. *A watch that allows you to send email* is a much clearer description than *an IP-enabled wristwatch.* One trick is to write the way you talk. If something doesn't sound right when you read it out loud, change it.

Avoid jargon.   Jargon is vocabulary that is specific to an industry or group of people. Because specialized language and technical terms can be confusing, it's best to avoid them, even for the savviest of audiences. Try this as a guideline: Use jargon only if you are completely confident that nearly every one of your readers – say, nine out of ten – will understand it.

In addition, certain words and phrases come in and out of fashion. Because not everyone will understand them, and they might mean different things to different people, try to avoid them. Faddish words and phrases include:

actionable items	bottom line (as noun or verb)
cutting edge	deliverables
dialogue (as a verb)	hands on
interface (as a verb)	proactive
repurpose	skill set

Don't hedge. Don't use wishy-washy language because you don't know exactly what you want to say or because you fear people will disagree with you.

The following words and phrases are red flags that you are hedging:

practically	Pretty
probably	Rather
seemingly	Somewhat
very	Virtually
as I recall	as I understand it
for all intents and purposes	I imagine
I would guess that	in some cases
is considered to be	it is my observation that
it is my opinion that	for the most part

may or may not be	my best guess is that
to the best of my recollection	under the circumstances

Use active rather than passive voice. In a sentence in the active voice, the subject performs the action. In a sentence in the passive voice, the subject receives the action.

> *Active voice:* We paid close attention to the consumers' comments.
> *Passive voice:* Close attention was paid to the consumers' comments.

Sentences in the passive voice tend to be duller, longer, and harder to understand than those in the active voice. They use forms of the helping verb *to be (is, was, were, has been, have been, shall be, will be, shall have been, will have been)* and phrases beginning with *by*. Active voice, in contrast, makes writing more energetic and forceful. *I used the active voice to write this book* sounds better than *The active voice was used by me in writing this book.*

If you can't figure out how to put an idea into active voice, figure out who or what is doing the action and make that the subject of the sentence. To identify sentences in passive voice, look for those helping verbs and phrases beginning with *by*.

There is one instance in which you might want to use passive voice on purpose: when you are trying to de-emphasize the subject. If you'd like to highlight something other than the subject – the action, for example – passive voice can be a good choice:

> *He was born on January 3, 1972.*
> *The employees were laid off during the third quarter.*

In all other cases, avoid passive voice.

Provide guideposts for your reader. Help your reader by providing signals and guideposts. Transitional words and phrases (such as *and, furthermore, even so,* and *therefore*) work to connect your thoughts and indicate what's to come. Another way to create transitions is to repeat a word or a phrase from the preceding paragraph.

When a paragraph or section contains several different points, numbering them (*first, second,* etc.) makes them clearer. Headers, lists, and bullets also help organize your thoughts for the reader.

Finally, make your reader's job easier by following the principle of parallel construction. Parallel construction means beginning each item in a list with the same part of speech (*the art of advertising, the science of accounting, and the mystery of marketing* – each item begins with a noun). This helps alert readers to the similarities or connections between things. If you introduce words or phrases with a preposition, include the preposition either only with the first item or with each of the items.

> *Parallel:* This book is for investors, managers, salespeople, and executives.
> *Parallel:* This book is for investors, for managers, for salespeople, and for executives.
> *Not parallel:* This book is for investors, managers, salespeople, and for executives.

It also helps to put related words together:

> *Confusing:* Investors in the 1930s hurt by the crash acted cautiously.
> *Better:* Investors hurt by the crash in the 1930s acted cautiously.

This kind of positioning makes sentences easier to understand.

Use strong endings. Use firm endings; don't go on and on and weaken your point. Use direct, strong statements. End by restating your major points or the benefits of following your recommendations.

Let it sit for a while. If possible, let your writing sit overnight. At least, an hour or two away from the document will allow you to approach it with a fresh eye and to edit more effectively.

Separate editing from writing. With writing, it's best to get your thoughts out rather than agonize over every detail.

Don't rely on a grammar- or spell-checker. Edit and review your documents yourself, and don't rely on a grammar- or spell-checker. In particular, a spell-checker won't recognize a legitimate word used incorrectly (*to* vs. *too,* for example).

Proofread, proofread, proofread. You can't proofread something too many times.

When in doubt, just start writing. If all of this seems too difficult, just start writing. As long as you have a basic idea of what you want to say, you can organize and polish later.

Top 5 Business Writing Tips

1. **Know why you're writing.** Before you begin writing, know what you want to say – and why you want to say it. One way to ensure you know why you're writing is to make an outline of your main points beforehand.

2. **Present the most important points first.** Present the most important point(s) at the beginning of your document; then use the paragraphs and sections that follow to support your statement. The same goes for paragraphs: At the beginning of each paragraph, state the main point. Then present the supporting details.

3. **Use simple, specific language.** Don't use a big word or an obscure word when a short word or a simple word will suffice. Choose concrete words and specific examples over abstract, vague language. Avoid technical jargon and clichés.

4. **Use active rather than passive voice.** Active voice makes writing more energetic and forceful. If you can't figure out how to put an idea into active voice, figure out who or what is doing the action and make that the subject of the sentence.

5. **Proofread, proofread, proofread.** You can't proofread something too many times. Do it yourself, and don't rely on spell- or grammar-check.

24

Getting Grammar Straight

Getting Grammar Straight

agreement   Pronouns must agree with the word they refer to in person, number, and gender. This is known as pronoun-antecedent agreement.

> *Incorrect:* Everyone wanted to cash in their stock options.
> *Correct:* Everyone wanted to cash in his or her stock options.
> (*Everyone* is singular; therefore, the pronouns that refer to it must be singular as well.)

Similarly, verbs must agree with the subject of the sentence. (If the subject is singular, the verb must be singular; if the subject is plural, the verb must be plural.) This is known as subject-verb agreement. Do not fall into the trap of making the verb agree with the noun closest to it if that noun is not the subject.

> *Incorrect:* A portion of our efforts are devoted to marketing.
> *Correct:* A portion of our efforts is devoted to marketing.
> (*Portion*, not *efforts*, which is the object of the prepositional phrase beginning with *of*, is the subject of the sentence. *Portion* is singular, so the verb must be singular.)

See also **subject/verb agreement.**

an   Use the article *an* when the word that follows starts with a vowel *sound*. Pay attention not to whether the first letter is actually a vowel or consonant, but what it *sounds* like:

> *an option*

an hourly wage
But: *a used book* (because the *u* sounds like a *y*)

and   *And* can be used to join words, phrases, and clauses.

> *To join words:* He is a pompous and arrogant man.
> *To join phrases:* We look for employees with outgoing personalities, the ability to solve problems quickly, and experience in the service industry.
> *To join clauses:* I like to dance, he likes to cook, and she likes to paint.

When using *and* to join two independent clauses, make sure the two clauses are equal in importance. Do not use *and* simply to tack on information at the end of a sentence or if one idea is dependent on another. (In the latter case, use a more specific word, such as *because* or *so*.)

> *Not good:* The shareholders' meeting was in Houston, Texas, and many people attended.
> *Better:* The shareholders' meeting, which many people attended, was in Houston, Texas.
> *Better:* The shareholders' meeting was in Houston, Texas. Many people attended.

> *Not good:* His plane was late, and he missed the meeting.
> *Better:* His plane was late, so he missed the meeting.

apostrophe (')   Use an apostrophe:

❏   When indicating possession: *a person's signature, people's signatures; the boy's toy, the boys' toys.*

When a singular common noun ends in *s*, add an *'s* (*princess's, boss's*) unless the word that follows also begins with *s* (*the boss' son*). For singular proper names

27

ending in *s*, use an apostrophe only *(Paris' food, Jesus' example)*.

For compound words, add apostrophe or *'s* to the word closest to the object possessed (*the vice president's opinion*).

❏ When indicating omitted letters or numerals: *can't, '90s*.

When an apostrophe appears in front of a number, it should face this way: '

Do not use an apostrophe:

❏ When forming the plural of numbers or decades: *1870s, 1990s; 20s, 30s, 40s*, etc.

❏ When forming the plural of letters or abbreviations: *Ds, Fs, VIPs*.

but, used at the beginning of a sentence   Contrary to popular belief, it is acceptable to use *but* at the beginning of a sentence. However, as with any other sentence formation, be careful not to overuse.

capitalization   Capitalize the first word of a sentence. This rule holds true when a sentence appears within a sentence (quoted material) or when a complete sentence follows a colon.

> *I couldn't believe it when she said, "Take the rest of the day off."*
> *Later, I found out why she gave us a vacation day: She didn't want us around while she was firing people.*

Capitalize titles only when they precede a person's specific name:

28

> *We heard President Bush speak.*
> *We heard the president speak.*

Capitalize the official names of governments, companies, and organizations. Do not capitalize common nouns such as *division, committee, manager, department,* and *director.* However, it's better to follow the conventions of your company and overcapitalize than to be a stickler about this.

Capitalize the trademarked names of products, but not the products themselves.

> *Band-Aid, bandage*
> *Kleenex, tissue*
> *Xerox, photocopy*

Capitalize the words *north, south, east,* and *west* only when they designate a well-known region (*the Midwest, Southern California*). Do not capitalize them when they indicate direction. *(The storm is moving north.)* Do not capitalize seasons of the year: *spring, autumn, winter, summer.*

Capitalize titles of books, articles, plays, and films. Do not capitalize articles, conjunctions, or short prepositions in titles *(A Man for All Seasons)* unless they begin or end the title *(In the Bedroom).* Capitalize prepositions that contain more than four letters *(A River Runs Through It).*

colon (:) Use a colon:

❑ To introduce a list of items. (*This report is missing several sections: a table of contents, an introduction, and a conclusion.*)

❑ To introduce an explanation. (*I'm not sure I agree with his conclusion: His logic seems flawed.*)

❑ To heighten the impact of the word or words that follow. (*The cause of her illness was simple: malnutrition.*)

❑ After the salutation of a business letter. (*Dear Mr. Smith:*)

❑ To separate elements of time (hours and minutes, minutes and seconds). (*The meeting starts at 3:30. Her official time for the race was 6:02:27.*)

Do not place a colon between a verb and its objects or between a preposition and its objects.

> *Incorrect:* Please address the letter to: the client, the CEO, and the lawyers.
> *Correct:* Please address the letter to the client, the CEO, and the lawyers.
> *Incorrect:* Our strongest departments are: accounting, marketing, and human resources.
> *Correct:* Our strongest departments are accounting, marketing, and human resources.

See also **quotation marks** for placement with quotes.

comma (,) Place a comma:

❑ Between two or more adjectives that modify a noun.

> *A dark, conservative suit is best for a job interview.*

❑ Between items in a series. The comma before the *and* or *or* in a series is now considered optional, but I include it to avoid confusion. Whether or not you choose to include this serial comma, be consistent throughout your document.

> *The flag is red, white, and blue.*

❏ To set off clauses that would not change the meaning of their subject if they were left out ("nonessential clauses"). If the words are essential to the meaning of the subject, do not enclose them in commas.

> *The conference room, which is comfortable but elegant, can hold 30 people.*

❏ Before a conjunction separating two independent clauses. However, if the clauses are extremely short, no comma is necessary.

> *She writes the documents within three to four weeks, and I edit them within a few days.*
> *She writes and I edit.*

❏ To separate a direct quote from the rest of the sentence.

> *"This report is pathetic," he yelled.*

❏ Between parts of dates and place names.

> *The agreement was signed on November 6, 2002, but didn't take effect until a month later.*
> *She will retire to Palm Beach, Florida, when she turns 70.*

❏ Between names and titles or degrees that follow.

> *Thomas Matthews, Jr.*
> *Angela Adams, M.D.*

See also **quotation marks** for placement with quotes.

comma splice Do not connect two individual sentences (known as independent clauses), each with its own subject and verb, by a comma. Instead, separate them with a semicolon or a period. If the clauses are short, you can also join them with a conjunction.

> *Incorrect:* Yesterday's meeting was there, today's meeting is here.
> *Correct:* Yesterday's meeting was there; today's meeting is here.
> *Correct:* Yesterday's meeting was there. Today's meeting is here.
> *Correct:* Yesterday's meeting was there, while today's meeting is here.

compound adjective See **hyphen.**

dangling modifiers Modifiers are words or phrases that define or alter the meaning of something. Modifiers are dangling when they don't modify the subject of the sentence.

> *Incorrect:* Believing the product to be faulty, it was recalled. (Who believes the product to be faulty?)
> *Correct:* Believing the product to be faulty, the company recalled it. (The company believes the product to be faulty.)

dash (–) The dash is used to interrupt or highlight an idea. (*My father – an accomplished golfer in his own right – never beat my mother in golf.*) Used most often in informal contexts, the dash should be used sparingly in business writing.

If you must use a dash and can't create one with the "function" option on your computer, use two hyphens with a space on either side (--).

32

either/or, neither/nor   *Either* goes with *or*; *neither* goes with *nor*.

> *Correct:* Neither the radio nor the television is working.
> *Correct:* I wish either the radio or the television were working.
> *Incorrect:* Neither the radio or the television is working.

ellipses (...)   Ellipses indicate that a word, phrase, sentence, or paragraph has been omitted. They are usually used in quoted material. Ellipses can appear at the beginning, middle, or end of a sentence.

The correct way to format ellipses is to use three dots with a space on either side. When deleted words come at the end of a sentence, use a fourth dot as the period.

Do not use ellipses for any other reason than to show omission.

exclamation point (!)   The exclamation point is used to show extreme emotion. Use only rarely; a period will almost always suffice.

See also **quotation marks** for placement with quotes.

fragment   A sentence is a group of words with a subject and a verb that form a complete thought. A sentence fragment is a group of words that does not form a complete thought.

> *Incorrect:* The stenographer typed. As fast as he could.
> (*As fast as he could* is not a complete sentence.)
> *Correct:* The stenographer typed as fast as he could.

Eliminate fragments from your writing.

hyphen (-)   Use hyphens when you combine two or more words to form an adjective or to create a new word or modifying phrase. Here's a good rule of thumb: If the reader might otherwise be confused, use a hyphen.

> *carry-on luggage*
> *day-by-day propositions*
> *the first-time traveler*
> *the first time-traveler*

If one of the words in a modifier is an adverb ending in *-ly*, do not use a hyphen.

> *She was fancily dressed.*

When a series of modifiers all end with the same word, the word needs only to appear at the end of the series.

> *We manufacture small-, large- and mid-size cars.*

italics   Italicize names of books, newspapers, magazines, periodicals, movies, and TV shows. Use quotation marks for titles of chapters, articles, reports, poems, songs, and musical works. Exception: The titles of long musical works and poems (for example, *Paradise Lost*) are italicized.

Italics may also be used to show emphasis. Use them sparingly for this purpose, however.

parallel construction   Parallel construction means beginning each item in a list with the same part of speech (*the art of advertising, the science of accounting, and the mystery of marketing* – each item begins with a noun). This helps alert readers to the similarities or connections between things. If you introduce words or phrases with a preposition, either include the preposition only with the first item or with each of the items.

> *Parallel:* This book is for investors, managers, salespeople, and executives.
> *Parallel:* This book is for investors, for managers, for salespeople, and for executives.
> *Not parallel:* This book is for investors, managers, salespeople, and for executives.

parentheses ( ) Parentheses are traditionally used to enclose explanatory material that's tangential to the main idea. They're also used to introduce an acronym or an abbreviation.

Try to limit the first use of parentheses: When you're tempted to use parentheses to enclose a tangential idea, consider how important the idea is. If it's important enough to be in the document, it probably doesn't belong in parentheses. If it's not important, it probably doesn't belong in the document.

Punctuation and parentheses: Put a period inside the closing parenthesis if the statement inside is a complete sentence. Otherwise, punctuate the sentence as if the parentheses did not exist.

> *Ice cream is my favorite dessert. (And chocolate is my favorite flavor.)*
> *Ice cream is my favorite dessert (especially chocolate).*

Note: Do not follow the written version of a number with a numeral in parentheses.

> *Incorrect:* Enclosed are three (3) documents.

period (.) Use a period:

❏   At the end of a sentence.

❑ In certain abbreviations: *a.m., p.m., B.A., M.A., Ph.D., M.D., Jr. Esq., Ms., Mrs., Mr., Bros., Co., Inc., U.S.A.* If an abbreviation ends a sentence, no additional period is needed.

> *At age 45, she went back to school to earn her Ph.D.*

See also **quotation marks** for placement with quotes.

person   See **point of view.**

point of view   When writing a document, adopt a point of view: *I* or *we* (first person); *you* (second person); or *he, she, it,* and *they* (third person). In documents on company stationery, *we* usually indicates the view of the company, while *I* indicates personal opinion.

Any of the three points of view is acceptable; just make sure not to shift person in the middle of a sentence or document.

prepositions   Are prepositions something you can end a sentence with? Yes. Most grammarians now disregard the old rule about not ending sentences with prepositions. It's better to end a sentence with a preposition than write an awkward, stilted statement.

> *Awkward:* This is the manual with which the computer
>   came.
> *Better:* This is the manual the computer came with.

pronouns   Pronouns are substitutes for nouns (or other pronouns). The key in understanding how to use pronouns is knowing whether they are subjects or objects in their sentences. When the pronoun is part of the subject of a sentence, use a nominative pronoun (see below). When the pronoun is part of the object in a sentence – the thing acted upon – or the object of a preposition, use the objective case.

Nominative	Objective
I/we	Me/us
You	You
He/she/it	Him/her/it
They	Them

A pronoun that follows a preposition is the object of that preposition and should therefore be in the objective case.

>*Correct:* It was I who wrote the report.
>*Incorrect:* It was me who wrote the report.

>*Correct:* Let's keep this between you and me.
>*Incorrect:* Let's keep this between you and I.

Another point about pronouns: Be clear about which noun they're replacing.

>*Ambiguous:* After Rick spoke to the man, he felt better. (Who felt better? Rick or the man?)
>*Clear:* After speaking with the man, Rick felt better.
>*Clear:* After Rick spoke with the man, Rick felt better. (It's better to repeat the noun and sound repetitive than to be unclear.)

One way to reduce confusion is to place the pronoun as close as possible to the noun it is replacing.

quotation marks (" ") The main function of quotation marks is to signal the beginning and end of a direct quote: *"Tell my husband I'll call him back," the CEO said to her secretary.* Also use quotation marks:

❏ Around the titles of articles, stories, speeches, and chapters and other parts of a larger printed work

❑ When introducing a new term *(We're calling our new toy a "zigley.")*

Punctuating with quotation marks: Many people find the question of whether to place periods and other punctuation inside or outside quotation marks confusing. The rules are simple:

❑ Periods and commas go inside the final quotation mark.

❑ Semicolons and colons go outside the final quotation mark.

❑ Question marks and exclamation points go inside the final quotation mark when they are part of the quoted material; they go outside the quotation mark when they are not.

> *Incorrect:* After the sales pitch he asked, "So how much will this really cost us"?
> *Correct:* After the sales pitch he asked, "So how much will this really cost us?"

Quotes within quotes: Use single quotation marks to note quotations within quotations.

> *The manager said, "During our presentation, I overheard the client say, 'I'm impressed.'"*

Do not use quotation marks to indicate that you are being sarcastic or using a word loosely.

> *Incorrect:* She thought the top made her look "with it."

run-on sentence A run-on sentence is two or more sentences without punctuation separating them.

> *The economy is good however the market for our product is poor.*

Ways to fix run-on sentences include:

❏ Dividing them into separate sentences.

> *The economy is good. However, the market for our product is poor.*

❏ Joining them with a comma and a conjunction.

> *The economy is good, but the market for our product is poor.*

❏ Joining them with a semicolon.

> *The economy is good; however, the market for our product is poor.*

semicolon (;)   The semicolon has two main uses:

❏ To connect two closely related sentences that are not joined by a conjunction.

> *Red is my favorite color; half my wardrobe is red.*

❏ To separate items on a list when the items are long, complex, or have commas within them.

> *I will need the following: two highlighters, one yellow and one green; three pencils; poster board, preferably the thick kind; and a large roll of masking tape.*

See also **quotation marks** for placement with quotes.

serial comma   The comma before the *and* or *or* in a series is now considered optional, but I include it to avoid confusion. Whether or not you choose to include this serial comma, be consistent throughout your document. See also **comma.**

split infinitive   Splitting infinitives is no longer a cardinal sin of grammar. Splitting an infinitive is preferable to creating an awkward-sounding sentence or leaving the meaning unclear. Most sentences, however, will sound natural without splitting infinitives.

> *Unclear:* It was difficult to understand actually what she was saying. (To actually understand, or what she was actually saying?)
> *Better:* It was difficult to actually understand what she was saying.

> *Unnecessary split:* To effectively communicate, you must be a competent writer.
> *Better:* To communicate effectively, you must be a competent writer.

subject/verb agreement   Singular subjects take singular verbs. Plural subjects take plural verbs.

This rule seems simple enough. Nonetheless, placing a singular noun with a plural verb is a common grammar mistake. Part of the problem is that many singular nouns seem as if they are plural: *Group, staff, board committee,* and *majority* are singular (and take singular verbs), for example.
> *Incorrect:* The staff are on vacation.
> *Correct:* The staff is on vacation.

Other nouns that are singular but often used mistakenly with plural verb forms include *each, everybody, everyone, anybody, somebody, someone, no one, either*, and *neither*. Many of these words incorporate the word *one* or *body*, which serves as a reminder that they refer to *one* person or thing.

Another common mistake is matching the verb with the word closest to it, rather than the actual subject of the sentence.

> *Incorrect:* The group of accountants are meeting at the hotel. (*Of accountants* is a prepositional phrase; *group,* a singular noun, is the subject of the sentence.)
> *Correct:* The group is meeting at the hotel.

> *Incorrect:* The majority [of people] are going to vote for a pay raise.
> *Correct:* The majority is going to vote for a pay raise. (If you mentally delete the prepositional phrase *of people,* it's easier to see that the subject of the sentence is *majority,* which is singular.)

If two singular parts of a subject are connected by *and*, the subject is plural and takes a plural verb.

> *Eating and drinking are two of my favorite pastimes.*

When two singular subjects are joined by *or,* the verb is singular.

> *Bob or Joyce is taking pledges today.*

When one part of a subject is singular and the other is plural and they are joined by *or,* the verb should agree with the part of the subject closest to it.

> *John or his friends are going to the mall.*
> *Either John's friends or John is representing the group.*

When subjects connected by *and* are commonly thought of as one item, the verb is singular.

> *Bacon and eggs is my favorite breakfast.*

See also **agreement.**

subjunctive   The phrase *If I were you* includes a subjunctive verb. Knowing the verb is subjunctive is not important, but it is important to know when to use *was* and when to use *were.*

Use *were* when an *if* clause states a situation that is impossible, extremely unlikely, or simply untrue. Use *was* in all other cases.

> *If I were you, I would make that phone call.* (It is impossible for me to be you.)
> *If I was asked, I'd go with you.* (It is possible that I'll be asked.)

titles   Italicize names of books, newspapers, magazines, periodicals, movies, and TV shows. Use quotation marks for titles of chapters, articles, reports, poems, songs, and musical works. Do not capitalize articles and conjunctions of three words or less (*The Times of London*).

Capitalize titles only when they precede a person's name.

> *President Bush's address*
> *the president's address*

See also **capitalization, italics,** and **quotation marks**.

Top 10 Grammar Mistakes

1. **Agreement errors**   Pronouns must agree with the word they refer to in person, number, and gender.

   > *Incorrect:* Everyone wanted to cash in their stock options.
   > *Correct:* Everyone wanted to cash in his or her stock options.

   Singular subjects take singular verbs. Plural subjects take plural verbs. *Each, everybody, everyone, anybody, somebody, someone, no one, either,* and *neither* are singular words that are often mistakenly used with plural verbs. *Group, staff, board, committee,* and *majority* are also singular.

   > *Incorrect:* The staff are on vacation.
   > *Correct:* The staff is on vacation.

2. **Comma splices**   Do not connect two individual sentences, each with its own subject and verb, by a comma.

   > *Incorrect:* Yesterday's meeting was there, today's meeting is here.
   > *Correct:* Yesterday's meeting was there. Today's meeting is here.

3. **Dangling modifiers**   Modifiers are words or phrases that define or alter the meaning of something. Modifiers are dangling when they don't modify the subject of the sentence.

Incorrect: Believing the product to be faulty, it was recalled. (Who believes the product to be faulty?)

Correct: Believing the product to be faulty, the company recalled it. (The company believes the product to be faulty.)

4. **Extra apostrophes**   Do not use an apostrophe to form the plurals of numbers or decades: *1870s, 1990s; 20s, 30s, 40s.* Use an apostrophe when numbers are missing, but make sure the apostrophe faces the right way: *the '70s.*

5. **Misplaced colons**   Do not place a colon between a verb and its objects or between a preposition and its objects.

> *Incorrect:* Please address the letter to: the client, the CEO, and the lawyers.
>
> *Correct:* Please address the letter to the client, the CEO, and the lawyers.

> *Incorrect:* Our strongest departments are: accounting, marketing, and human resources.
>
> *Correct:* Our strongest departments are accounting, marketing, and human resources.

6. **Incorrect punctuation with parentheses**   Put a period inside the closing parenthesis if the statement inside is a complete sentence. Otherwise, punctuate the sentence as if the parentheses do not exist.

> *Ice cream is my favorite dessert. (And chocolate is my favorite flavor.)*
>
> *Ice cream is my favorite dessert (especially chocolate).*

44

7. **Misused pronouns** A pronoun that follows a preposition is the object of that preposition and should therefore be in the objective case.

    Correct: Let's keep this between you and me.
    Incorrect: Let's keep this between you and I.

8. **Incorrect punctuation with quotation marks** Periods and commas go inside the final quotation mark. Semicolons and colons go outside the final quotation mark. Question marks and exclamation points go inside the final quotation mark when they are part of the quoted material and outside when they are not.

    Incorrect: After the sales pitch he asked, "So how much will this really cost us"?
    Correct: After the sales pitch he asked, "So how much will this really cost us?"

9. **Run-on sentences** A run-on sentence is two or more sentences without punctuation separating them.

    Incorrect: The economy is good however the market for our product is poor.
    Correct: The economy is good; however, the market for our product is poor.

10. **Sentence fragments** A sentence fragment is a group of words that do not form a complete thought.

    Incorrect: The stenographer typed. As fast as he could. (*As fast as he could* is not a complete sentence.)
    Correct: The stenographer typed as fast as he could.

Dealing With Questions of Style

Abbreviation, Capitalization, and Other Information

aboveboard   One word, no hyphen.

Abbreviations   Use abbreviations sparingly, unless you are certain the reader knows what they stand for.

Some words, however, are almost always abbreviated. They include *a.m., p.m., B.C., A.D., Mr., Mrs., Ms.,* and *Dr.* When they follow a person's name, *Jr.* and *Sr.* are also abbreviated.

Use an ampersand (*&*) in place of *and* and abbreviate the words *Brothers* (Bros.), *Company (Co.), Corporation (Corp.),* and *Incorporated (Inc.)* when they are part of a company's formal name. When not used as part of a name, spell out these words.

Do not abbreviate months, days of the week, or the words *street, avenue, road,* and *boulevard.* Do not abbreviate the names of states except in postal addresses.

Acronyms   Like abbreviations, acronyms should be used sparingly, unless you are certain the reader knows what they stand for. Write out a word the first time you use it and note its acronym in parentheses. From then on, you may use the acronym alone.

Ad-lib   Hyphenated in all of its forms: adjective, noun, and verb.

a.k.a. (also known as)   Punctuate with periods; use lowercase.

Ages   Use numerals when indicating age, even if the age is under ten. This is an exception to the rule about when to use numerals and words on Page 70.

> *Our fleet of airplanes is 7 years old.*

Hyphenate ages when they are used as adjectives or replacements for nouns; otherwise, no hyphen is necessary.

> *I have a 6-year-old daughter.*
> *My daughter is 6 years old.*
> *This toy is designed for 6-year-olds.*

Do not use an apostrophe in the following constructions: *20s, 30s, 40s,* etc.

> *Most of the middle managers are in their 30s.*

a.m., p.m.   Lowercase with periods. Note that *6 p.m. in the evening* is redundant. The use of *a.m.* or *p.m.* already indicates time of day.

Ampersand (&)   Do not use in place of *and* unless the ampersand is part of an organization's formal name.

And/or   Confusing to the reader; avoid. Also avoid *either/or, he/she*, and similar expressions with slashes.

Apostrophes   Do not use apostrophes when writing the plural of an abbreviation. Do not use apostrophes in the following constructions: *1870s, 1990s; 20s, 30s, 40s,* etc.

> *Most of the middle managers are in their 30s.*

See also **apostrophe** in Chapter 2.

Board   Do not capitalize unless the word is part of an organization's full, official name.

> *I'll have to discuss your proposal with the board before
> making a decision.*
> *We're presenting our proposal to the Cincinnati Board
> of Trade tomorrow.*

Board of directors, board of trustees Do not capitalize in generic uses. Capitalize in internal correspondence if that is the company's custom. See also **titles.**

Brand-new Hyphenate.

Brothers Abbreviate when part of formal company name.

> *Do you know where Warner Bros. Is based?*

Building Write out; do not abbreviate as *bldg.*

Bullets There is no one correct way to punctuate bulleted items. If a bulleted item is a complete sentence, capitalize the first letter and end with the appropriate end punctuation (period, question mark). If the item is not a complete sentence, you may end with a period, comma, semicolon, or nothing at all – but be consistent. It's still a good idea to capitalize the first word in each bullet.

Bureau Capitalize only when part of an organization's formal name.

Cents Use numerals and spell out the word *cents* (*8 cents, 60 cents*). This is an exception to the rule about when to use words and when to use numerals on Page 70.

Century Hyphenate when used with another word to form an adjective. Do not hyphenate when used as a noun.

> *The Internet is a 20th-century phenomenon.*
> *People started using the Internet in the 20th century.*

Note that the century designation does not correspond with a century's years: The 20th century began in 1900, not 2000.

Chairman, chairwoman, chairperson   Capitalize only as a formal title that appears before a person's name: *company Chairman Bill Gates.* Do not capitalize when referring to a less formal, temporary position: *chairperson of the improvement committee Joe Smith.*

Chapter numbers   Can be written as words or numerals. (*Chapter 3* and *Chapter Three* are both correct.)

city   Capitalize only when part of an official name or nickname; otherwise, lowercase: *New York City; the city of Los Angeles; Chicago, the Windy City.*

Committee   *Committee* is a singular noun that takes a singular verb.

Company   If a business ends its proper name with *Company* or *Companies*, abbreviate as *Co.* or *Cos.* (Possessive: *Co.'s* and *Cos.'*) If either word is used alone, do not abbreviate.

Company names   See *Standard & Poor's Register of Corporations* or consult the company itself for a company's exact name. Put a comma before *Inc.* or *Ltd.* And a comma after *Inc.* or *Ltd.* If they do not end the sentence.

Corporation   Abbreviate as *Corp.* when used at the end of an organization's formal name. Do not abbreviate when used alone.

Data   *Data* is technically the plural form of the word *datum.* However, it has become acceptable to use *data* with a singular verb in all but the most formal contexts.

Formal: The data *show* we are heading in the right direction.
Informal: The data *shows* we are heading in the right direction.

Dates   Punctuate dates as follows: *September 4, 1973.* When a complete date appears in the middle of a sentence, it is followed by a comma. When only a month and year appear, no comma is necessary.

> *The author was born on September 4, 1973, in Washington, D.C.*
> *September 1973 was hot and humid in Washington, D.C.*

International correspondence: Many countries other than the United States express dates as follows: 4 September 1973, and 4/9/73. Keep this in mind when using numerical forms for dates (9/4/73 in the United States), so the month and day are not confused.

Daylong   One word, no hyphen. Same holds true for *weeklong, monthlong,* and *yearlong.*

Decade   Write as follows: *1990s, '90s, mid-1990s.* Use apostrophe when writing *'90s* because numbers have been omitted (note direction of apostrophe: ' and not '). Do not use apostrophe when writing *1990s* because no numbers have been omitted. See **apostrophe** Page 32.

Depression   Capitalize only when referring to the *Great Depression.*

Director   Capitalize only as a formal title that appears before a person's name: *FBI Director J. Edgar Hoover.*

Distances   Follow the rules for numbers, Page 70. Write out one through ten; use numerals for numbers over ten.

The plant is five miles away.
The satellite office is 12 miles south of here.

Dollars   Use numerals when expressing dollar amounts *($2, $3,000)*. For amounts of $1 million or more, use numerals up to two decimals *($3.5 million)*. Do not hyphenate numerals with the words *million, billion,* etc. *($540 million deficit,* not *$540-million deficit)*.

Each   Use with a singular verb.

> *Each of the automobiles was a different color.*
> *Each of you is exceptionally qualified.*

Each and every   Redundant. Use *each* or *every.*

Either ... or, neither ... nor   *Either* should be used with *or; neither* should be used with *nor.* The verb should agree with the subject that is closer to it.

> *Either Jack or Jill is going to the meeting*
> *Neither the CEO nor the trustees are going to the meeting.*
> *Neither the trustees nor the CEO is going to the meeting.*

Email vs. **e-mail**   Experts disagree on whether to use a hyphen. Either follow company convention or choose one way and be consistent in all uses. *Special note for international correspondence:* In both French and German, *email*, without the hyphen, means enamel or glaze.

Fax   *Fax* is an acceptable abbreviation of the word *facsimile* in most contexts.

Firm Use *firm* when referring to a business partnership. Do not use when referring to an incorporated business; use *corporation* or *company* instead.

First, second, third Use *first, second, third*, etc., instead of *firstly, secondly, thirdly,* etc.

first quarter vs. **first-quarter** Do not hyphenate when used as a noun. (*The company did well during the first quarter.*) Hyphenate when used as an adjective. (*The first-quarter results were excellent.*)

fractions Spell out and hyphenate amounts less than 1 (*four-fifths*). Express as numerals when the amount is more than 1 (*6 ½ inches*). Use numerals for amounts larger than one (and convert to decimals when possible, but try to avoid mixing fractions and decimals in the same document).

Full- Hyphenate when used as an adjective (*full-scale initiative, full-time employee*).

Fund-raiser Hyphenate.

Fund-raising vs. **fund raising** Hyphenate when used as an adjective; do not hyphenate when used as a noun.

> *The fund-raising event is this evening at 8.*
> *Skillful fund raising is key to an organization's success.*

Gender Make every effort to ensure your language is gender-neutral, particularly when referring to professions. Here are some traditional names of occupations that are now considered sexist and their suggested replacements.

Replace:	With:
anchorman	anchor
chairman	chairperson, chair
fireman	firefighter
foreman	supervisor
housewife	homemaker
man (verb)	staff, operate
mankind	humankind, humanity
mailman	mail carrier
policeman	police officer
repairman	service technician
salesman	salesperson
spokesman	spokesperson
stewardess	flight attendant

See also **his, her.**

Girl Use until 18th birthday; then use *woman* or *young woman.*

Half Does not need to be used with the word *of. Half the group* and *half of the group* are both correct.

Headquarters Singular noun that takes a singular verb. *The company's headquarters is in Columbus, Ohio.*

Health care vs. **healthcare** Follow company convention or pick one and be consistent in all uses.

Height, width Use numerals and spell out words such as yards, feet, and inches. Hyphenate only when used as adjectives before nouns.

He is a 6-foot-7-inch basketball player.

He is 6 feet 7 inches tall.

High-tech   Hyphenate.

His, her   Do not use *he, him,* or *his* to represent both sexes. *She or he, him or her,* and *his or her* is acceptable but cumbersome.

There are several ways to avoid biased language without sounding awkward, including making the pronoun plural, using the pronoun *you,* using the pronoun *we,* using an article *(a, an, the),* using passive voice, and taking the pronoun out altogether.

> *Avoid:* A salesperson must know his client well.
> *Avoid:* A salesperson must know his or her client well.
> *Better:* As a salesperson, you must know your client well.
> *Better:* Salespeople must know their clients well.
> *Better:* A salesperson must know the client well.
> *Better:* As salespeople, we must know our clients well.
> *Better:* Clients must be well known by their salespeople.

Another option is to alternate the use of *his* and *her* throughout a document, using the masculine pronoun in one instance and the feminine pronoun in the next.

Incorporated   Abbreviate and capitalize as *Inc.* when part of a formal company name. Set off by commas: *Widget Makers, Inc.*

IOU, IOUs   Acceptable acronym in all instances. Do not use an apostrophe when forming the plural.

55

Italics Italicize names of books, newspapers, magazines, periodicals, movies, and TV shows. Use quotation marks for titles of chapters, articles, reports, poems, songs, and musical works. Exception: The titles of long musical works and poems *(e.g., Paradise Lost)* are italicized.

Italics may also be used to show emphasis. Use them sparingly for this purpose, however.

Italicize foreign words or phrases that have not become fully accepted as part of the English language. (Her *joie de vivre* motivated the entire committee. His *quid pro quo* was unacceptable.) Some foreign words have become so ingrained in the English language that they no longer need to be italicized (etc., bon voyage).

Jargon Jargon is vocabulary that is specific to an industry or group of people. Avoid.

Junior, senior Abbreviate as *Jr.* and *Sr.* when following a person's name. Set off by a comma: *John J. Beatty, Jr.*

languages Capitalize the names of languages: *French, Arabic, Japanese.*

Long-distance vs. **long distance** Hyphenate when used as an adjective; do not hyphenate when used as a noun. Same rule applies to *long-term* vs. *long term.*

> *His long-distance bill was high this month.*
> *They ran the long distance without stopping.*
> *Long-term care is expensive.*
> *We're in the stock market for the long term.*

Long time vs. **longtime** *Long time* is a noun; *longtime* is an adjective.

56

We haven't seen our friends in a long time.
Our longtime friends will visit us next weekend.

Magazine names   Capitalize and place in italics. Lowercase the word *magazine* unless it is part of the publication's official title.

Marketplace   One word, no hyphen.

Master of science, master of arts   May be abbreviated as *M.S.* and *M.A. Master's* or *master's degree in x* also acceptable.

Master of business administration   Commonly abbreviated as *M.B.A* or *MBA. Note:* It is becoming more acceptable to eliminate the periods in degrees; it certainly looks less cluttered in a biography, for instance, when the person has several degrees.

Measurements   See **height, width.**

Media   When used to describe the press, *media* is a plural noun and takes a plural verb. (The media are bombarding the candidate with questions.) Its misuse as a singular noun, however (usually by members of the media), is now so common that it is increasingly rare to hear the word used correctly.

> *Correct (but now rare):* The media are bombarding the candidate with questions.
> *Incorrect (but more common):* The media is bombarding the candidate with questions.

Memorandum, memorandums   Add *s* to form plural.

Middle-class vs. **middle class**   Hyphenate when used as an adjective; do not hyphenate when used as a noun.

She grew up in a middle-class neighborhood.
The tax cut will greatly benefit the middle class.

Middle initials   In general, use a person's middle initial(s).
Middle initials may be dropped if a person doesn't use one or
is commonly known without one.

Midnight, noon   Do not use *12* in front of them; redundant.

mix-up vs. **mix up**   Hyphenate when used as a noun; do not
hyphenate when used as a verb.

The mix-up made him miss his flight.
We mix up the name tags as part of the game.

Mock-up   Always hyphenated; used as a noun only.

Monthlong   One word. Same holds true for *daylong* and
yearlong.

Months   Capitalize and spell out. Exception: Months may be
abbreviated when used in lists, tables, or invoices.

Mr., Mrs., Ms.   *Mr.* refers to a man; *Mrs.* Refers to a married
woman; and *Ms.* Refers to either a married or a single woman.
Use *Ms.* When you are unsure of a woman's marital status.
The plural forms of *Mr.* and *Mrs.* Are *Messrs.* And *Mmes.*
There is no plural form of *Ms.*

Nationwide   One word. Same holds true for *statewide* and
citywide, as well as *companywide* and *officewide.*

Newspaper names   Capitalize and place in italics. Capitalize
and italicize *the* only if it is part of the formal title.

58

No.   Use as an abbreviation with a numeral to indicate rank: *No. 2 candidate.* Do not use in street addresses (Use # instead).

Noon, midnight   Do not use *12* in front of them; redundant.

North, south, east, west   Capitalize only when designating specific regions. *(The North was more industrialized than the South during the Civil War.)* Do not capitalize when indicating direction. *(Drive west until you reach the coast.)*

numbers   Spell out numbers ten and under; use numerals for numbers over ten.

> *We took ten baskets to the market.*
> *He will turn 11 tomorrow.*

Exception: Write out numbers that begin sentences, even if they are over ten. Use numerals in combination with the word *percent* and when referring to round numbers in the millions, billions, trillions, etc.

> *Twenty-one days was plenty of time to get the presentation together.*
> *Only about 10 percent of the presentation is completed.*

Exception: Use numerals when referring to addresses, dates, fractions, page numbers, and time of day (except when the word *o'clock* is used).

> *The recipe calls for 1 1/3 cup of molasses.*
> *I woke up at 7 a.m.*

Exception: Use numerals when expressing measurements:

> *My office is 8 feet by 14 feet.*

If you use more than one number in the same sentence, be consistent about either spelling the numbers out or using numerals.

>*Avoid:* Because we were so lax, we now have six days to prepare the presentation instead of 21.
>*Better:* Because we were so lax, we now have 6 days to prepare the presentation instead of 21.
>*Better:* Because we were so lax, we now have six days to prepare the presentation instead of twenty-one.

Off Not *off of.*

OK, Oks, OK'd, OK'ing Not *okay.* Avoid all forms of *OK* in formal documents.

Online One word, no hyphen.

p.m. See **a.m., p.m.**

page numbers Use numerals and capitalize the word *page* (*Page 3, Page 24*).

Part-time vs. **part time** Hyphenate when used as an adjective. Do not hyphenate when used as an adverb.

>*I'm thinking of getting a part-time job.*
>*When I worked part time, I had a bit more income.*

People Possessive form is *people's.*

per Use *per* to mean *for each, through,* or *by means of.* Do not use *per* to mean according to. The expression *as per* is also incorrect.

>*Correct:* He charges me $1.50 per pound.

> *Incorrect:* As per our conversation, I've contacted the distributor.

Percent   Spell out the word *percent* in combination with numerals (*3 percent, 17 percent*). *Exception:* The % symbol may be used in lists, tables, and invoices.

Ph.D., Ph.D.s   No apostrophe when forming the plural. (See note on *master of business administration,* Page 68.)

phenomenon, phenomena   *Phenomenon* is the singular form; *phenomena* is the plural.

> *Spontaneous combustion is an unusual phenomenon.*
> *The scientist told us about some of the phenomena he had seen over the years.*

Pigeonhole   One word, no hyphen.

Pipeline   One word, no hyphen.

Policy-maker, **policy-making**   Hyphenated when used as both noun and adjective.

Prefixes   Here are some general guidelines for punctuating prefixes:

Use a hyphen if the word that follows the prefix is capitalized (*anti-American, pro-Canadian*).

Use a hyphen if the prefix ends in a vowel and the word that follows it begins with the same vowel (*multi-industry*).

Use hyphen to join double prefixes (*sub-subcontractor*).
Do not hyphenate a prefix when the prefix ends in a vowel and the word that follows it begins with a consonant (*multimillionaire*).

Prefixes rarely follow fixed rules, however, so it's best to consult a dictionary. Punctuation guidelines for some of the quirkier prefixes follow:

all- Use a hyphen afterward *(all-star)*.

After- No hyphen afterward when used to create a noun *(afterthought)*; do use hyphen when used to create and adjective *(after-lunch* nap).

Co- Use a hyphen when forming a word that indicates occupation or status *(co-chairman, co-worker)*; otherwise, no hyphen *(coordinate, cooperate, coefficient)*.

Ex- Use hyphen when indicating *former*; no hyphen when indicating *out of (ex-president, excommunicate)*.

Extra- Use hyphen when indicating unusual size or extent; no hyphen when indicating *outside of (extra-large, extraordinary)*.

Pan- No hyphen when used with common nouns; usually takes a hyphen when used with proper nouns *(pantheism, pan-Asian)*.

Pro- Use hyphen to make words expressing support *(pro-choice, pro-labor)*. Otherwise, no hyphen.

Profit-sharing Hyphenate as both a noun and an adjective.

Ratios Use numerals and hyphens when expressing ratios *(a ratio of 3-to-2)*. Omit the word *to* when numerals precede the word *ratio (a 3-2 ratio)*.

Seasons Lowercase season names unless they are part of an official name.

> *I can't wait for summer.*

I can't wait for the Save for Summer sale to begin.

Serial comma   See **comma** and **serial comma,** Chapter 2.

Sexist language   See **gender** and **his, her.**

Software titles   Capitalize but don't put in quotation marks (*Microsoft Word*). Use quotation marks for computer games, however *("Primal Rage")*.

Speeches   Capitalize and put in quotation marks when using a speech's formal title.

Spokesman, spokeswoman, spokesperson   All are acceptable.

Springtime   One word, no hyphen. Same rule holds for *summertime* and *wintertime*.

State   Do not capitalize the word state when writing *the state of x*. Capitalize when part of a state's official name or nickname: *the state of New York, New York State, the Show-me State.*

State names   Capitalize and spell out state names when they occur within a sentence. Use postal service abbreviations (listed below, in parentheses) only when a full address, including zip code, is used.

Alabama (AL)	Montana (MT)
Alaska (AK)	Nebraska (NE)
Arizona (AZ)	Nevada (NV)
Arkansas (AR)	New Hampshire (NH)
California (CA)	New Jersey (NJ)
Colorado (CO)	New Mexico (NM)
Connecticut (CT)	New York (NY)
Delaware (DE)	North Carolina (NC)

Florida (FL)
Georgia (GA)
Hawaii (HI)
Idaho (ID)
Illinois (IL)
Indiana (IN)
Iowa (IA)
Kansas (KS)
Kentucky (KY)
Louisiana (LA)
Maine (ME)
Maryland (MD)
Massachusetts (MA)
Michigan (MI)
Minnesota (MN)
Mississippi (MS)
Missouri (MO)

North Dakota (ND)
Ohio (OH)
Oklahoma (OK)
Oregon (OR)
Pennsylvania (PA)
Rhode Island (RI)
South Carolina (SC)
South Dakota (SD)
Tennessee (TN)
Texas (TX)
Utah (UT)
Vermont (VT)
Virginia (VA)
Washington (WA)
West Virginia (WV)
Wisconsin (WI)
Wyoming (WY)

When a place is identified by city and state, place commas between the city and state and after the state:

> *He was born in Wichita, Kansas, and stayed there with his family all his life.*

Steppingstone   One word, no hyphen.

Street   Abbreviate as *St.* only when used in a postal address.
I live on Pollard Street.
Send the package to 535 Pollard St., Arlington, VA, 22203.

Suffixes   Like prefixes, suffixes are quirky, and it's best to check the dictionary. Here are punctuation guidelines for some of the most commonly used suffixes:

-fold   No hyphen (*threefold, sixfold*).

-less   No hyphen (*fearless, jobless*).

-like   No hyphen unless the *l* would be tripled (*businesslike, bell-like*).

-size   Hyphenate (*medium-size*).

Note: Do not use a hyphen between adjectives and adverbs ending in *–ly* (*easily missed*, not *easily-missed*).

Summertime   One word, no hyphen. Same rule holds for *wintertime* and *springtime*.

Table numbers   Use numerals and capitalize the word *table*. (*See Table 3, Page 27*).

Telephone numbers   Format as follows: (202) 361-1186, Ext. 3.

Telltale   One word, no hyphen.

That   *That* may be eliminated as long as the sentence remains clear without it. If eliminating *that* might create confusion, however, do not omit it.

> *Acceptable:* I think that those two companies might merge.
> *Acceptable:* I think those two companies might merge. (*that* omitted)
> *Avoid:* He does not see firing employees would hurt us.
> *Better:* He does not see that firing employees would hurt us.

3-D   Not three-D.

times   Format as follows: *6 a.m., 4:30 p.m.* Avoid redundancies such as *9 a.m. this morning* and *7 p.m. Tuesday evening.* Spell out the words *noon* and *midnight.*

Use numerals in combination with *a.m.* or *p.m.* Spell out numbers when they are followed by followed by *o'clock.*

Time zones   Capitalize when using the full name of a time zone: *Eastern Standard Time, Central Daylight Time.* Do not capitalize anything but the region when using shortened forms of time zones (*Mountain time*). Abbreviations are acceptable when used with a specific clock reading (*3 p.m. EST*).

titles   Italicize names of books, newspapers, magazines, periodicals, movies, and TV shows. Use quotation marks for titles of chapters, articles, reports, poems, songs, and musical works. Do not capitalize articles unless they are part of the official title and conjunctions of three words or less (*The Times of London*).

Capitalize titles only when they precede a specific person's name:

> *Former President Bill Clinton spoke at my college graduation.*
> *A former president spoke at my college graduation.*

See also **capitalization, italics**, and **quotation marks,** in Chapter 2.

Titleholder   One word, no hyphen.

TV   Acceptable as an adjective; avoid using as a noun. (*Television* is preferred.)

> *Which TV shows do you enjoy?*
> *I turn the television off when I'm eating.*

Under way   Two words.

United States, U.S.   Spell out *United States* as noun; use *U.S.* as adjective only.

> *The United States is negotiating for peace.*
> *The U.S. negotiations for peace are ongoing.*

Upstate   One word, no hyphen. Always lowercase.

Versus   Always abbreviate as *vs.*

VIP, VIPs   This acronym for *very important person(s)* is acceptable in most contexts.

Web page, Web site, website   *Web page* should be two words. Either *Web site* or *website* is acceptable.

Weeklong   One word, no hyphen. Same rule holds for *daylong*, *monthlong*, and *yearlong*.

Weight   Use figures and hyphenate in adjective form.

> *The product weighs 8 pounds, 3 ounces.*
> *The company makes an 8-pound, 3-ounce product.*

Well   Do not hyphenate a modifier that includes the word *well* when it comes after the word it modifies. Hyphenate when it precedes the word.

> *Her efforts were well intentioned.*
> *Her well-intentioned efforts were ignored.*

Whereabouts   Takes a singular verb: *Her whereabouts is unknown.*

White-collar   Hyphenate.

Wintertime   One word, no hyphen. Same holds true for *springtime* and *summertime*.

Word-of-mouth   Hyphenate.

Work force   Two words.

Workweek   One word, no hyphen.

Worldwide   One word, no hyphen. Same for *nationwide, countrywide, companywide, officewide*.

Worthwhile   One word, no hyphen.

Wrongdoing   One word, no hyphen.

Year-end   Hyphenate.

Yearlong   One word. Same for *daylong, weeklong, monthlong*.

Year   Follow the year with a comma if the year is part of a specific date in the middle of a sentence.

> *The CEO was born January 3, 1974, in Michigan.*

Do not use a comma if only a month and year are listed.

> *The CEO was born in January 1974 in Michigan.*

See also **decade.**

Yesteryear   One word, no hyphen.

Youth   Applies to boys and girls from ages 13 to 18. Use *man* or *woman* for people 18 and older.

Top 10 Style Tips

1. Use abbreviations and acronyms sparingly. When you do use them, tell the reader what they stand for the first time you mention them.

    > *The Federal Trade Commission (FTC) is responsible for issues of identity theft. We won't know how to proceed until an FTC representative contacts us.*

2. Punctuate dates as follows: *The author was born on September 4, 1973, in Washington, DC.* Write out the month (do not abbreviate), and place a comma after the year.

3. Write out numbers one through ten; use numerals for numbers over ten. However, use numerals when expressing ages, dollar amounts, measurements (height, width, weight), and percents.

4. Instead of using *his or her* in an effort to be gender neutral, try making the pronoun plural, eliminating the pronoun altogether, or using *you*.

    > *Avoid:* A salesperson must know his or her client.
    > *Better:* Salespeople must know their clients.

5. Do not capitalize *north, south, east,* and *west* when indicating direction. Capitalize only when referring to a specific region (*the Midwest*). Do not capitalize the names of seasons unless they are part of an official name.

6. Consult a dictionary when punctuating prefixes. Some general guidelines: Include a hyphen when the word that

follows the prefix is capitalized (*pro-Canadian*). Also hyphenate when the prefix ends in a vowel and the word that follows begins with the same vowel (*multi-industry*). Do not use a hyphen when the word that follows the prefix begins with a consonant (*multimillionaire*).

7. Write out the names of states except in postal addresses. When a place is identified by city and state, place commas between the city and state and after the state:

> *He was born in Wichita, Kansas, and stayed there most of his life.*

8. Format times as follows: *6 a.m., 4:30 p.m.* Avoid redundancies such as *6:30 a.m. this morning (a.m.* indicates morning already). Use numerals in combination with *a.m.* and *p.m.*; spell out numbers when they are followed by followed by *o'clock*.

9. Capitalize and italicize names of books, newspapers, magazines, periodicals, movies, and TV shows. Use quotation marks for titles of chapters, articles, reports, poems, songs, and musical works.

10. Capitalize titles only when they appear directly before a person's name: *President George W. Bush; George W. Bush, president of the United States.*

Avoiding Common Mistakes

Frequently Misspelled Words and Misused Terms

Frequently Misspelled Words
(spelled correctly here)

a lot (not alot)
accessible
accommodate
accumulate
accuracy
acknowledgment
acquaintance
acquire
ad nauseam
adjournment
advantageous
adviser (not advisor)
advisory
affidavit
affiliated
afterward (not afterwards)
aggravate
aggressive
align
all right (not alright)
alumnus, alumni (masculine); alumna,
alumnae (feminine)
amateur
amid (not amidst)
among (not amongst)
analyze
analysis
anonymous

apparatus
apparent
applicable
apropos
ascertain
auxiliary
ax (not axe), axed,
axing
bankruptcy
beneficial
bona fide
bookkeeping
brochure
bureau
business
calendar
cancellation
cannot (one word)
Caribbean
changeable
changeover
chargeable
Cincinnati
clientele
column
committee
comparative
comptroller

Connecticut
conscience
conscientious
conscious
correlate
counterfeit
consensus
contemptible
defendant
dependent
desperate
dilemma
diligence
disbursement
disillusioned
dissatisfied
egregious
embarrass
encyclopedia
endeavor
erroneous
exaggerate
existence
explanation
extraordinary
eye, eyed, eyeing
facilitate
facsimile
fascinate
feasible
flack vs. flak
financier
fluorescent
forward (not forwards)
gauge
grievance
guarantee

harass
homemade
humorous
inasmuch as
index, indexes,
indices
indispensable
installation
interrupt
jeopardy
judgment
justifiable
leisure
liaison
license
lieutenant
likable (not likeable)
maintenance
manageable
maneuver
meager
Mediterranean
memento (not
momento)
mileage
millennium
millionaire
minuscule (not miniscul
miscellaneous
mortgage
necessary
noticeable
nowadays (not
nowdays)
obsession
occasion
occurred

occurrence
omission
opportunity
pageant
permanent
permissible
persistent
possession
posthumous
potato, potatoes
precede
prejudice
prescription
prevalent
prima-facie
privilege
proviso, provisos
questionnaire
recommend
referral
referred
relevant
remembrance
restaurateur
rhyme
rhythm
salable (preferred, although
saleable not incorrect)
sandwich
satisfactorily
seize
separate
serviceable
simultaneous
sizable
subpoena
subtle

succeed
successor
supersede
supervisor
susceptible
suspicious
technique
tendency
Tennessee
total, totaled, totaling
toward (not towards)
transferring
twelfth
unanimous
unnecessary
upward (not upwards)
usable
vendor
veto, vetoes, vetoed,
vetoing
wholly
zero, zeroes

Frequently Misused Terms

ability vs. **capacity**   *Ability* is the state of being able to do something. *Capacity* is the potential for accommodating or containing.

about vs. **approximately**   *About* is more imprecise than *approximately*. *Approximately* means close to exact.

accept vs. **except**   *Accept* means to receive willingly. *Except* means excluding.

access vs. **excess**   *Access* means ability to approach. *Excess* means surplus.

actionable   This word has come into common misuse in business. It's strictly a legal term, an adjective that means giving cause for legal action or a lawsuit. It should not be used in business writing unless the writing refers to legal matters.

adverse vs. **averse**   *Adverse* means harmful or unfavorable. *Averse* means feeling distaste.

advice vs. **advise**   *Advice* (noun) means opinion about what could or should be done. *Advise* (verb) means to offer suggestions.

advise vs. **inform**   *Advise* means to offer suggestions. *Inform* means to communicate knowledge.

adopt vs. **adapt**   *Adopt* means to take as one's own. *Adapt* means to adjust.

affect vs. **effect**   *Affect* (verb) means to influence or change. *Effect* means to bring about (verb) or result (noun).

> *That movie affected me quite a bit.*
> *The effect of that movie was powerful.*

all ready vs. **already**   *All ready* means prepared. *Already* means previously.

all together vs. **altogether**   *All together* means in unison. *Altogether* means completely.

allude vs. **elude**   *Allude* means to refer to indirectly. *Elude* means to avoid or escape.

allude vs. **refer**   *Allude* means to refer to indirectly. *Refer* indicates a direct reference.

allusion vs. **illusion**   *Allusion* is indirect reference or hint. *Illusion* is an incorrect perception.

altar vs. **alter**   *Altar* is a sacred table. *Alter* is to change.

alternate vs. alternative   *Alternate* means substitute (adj.) or a substitute (noun). *Alternative* means offering a choice (adj.) or a situation offering a choice of two or more possibilities (noun).

among vs. **between**   *Between* introduces two items; *among* introduces more than two.

> *I am deciding between a red couch and a blue couch for the lobby.*
> *I think the tan couch is my favorite among the choices.*

amount vs. **number**   *Amount* refers to the quantity of something that cannot be counted in individual units (sugar, money). *Number* refers to something that can be counted in individual units (packages of sugar, dollars).

> *The amount of help we received was unprecedented.*
> *The number of people who helped was unprecedented.*

anyone vs. **any one**   *Anyone* is used as an indefinite reference. *Any one* is used when singling out a person or thing in a group.

appraise vs. **apprise**   *Appraise* means to judge the worth of. *Apprise* means to inform.

assure vs. **ensure** vs. **insure**   *Assure* means to guarantee or convince. *Ensure* mean to make secure or certain. *Insure* also means to make secure or certain but is used in the sense of securing the value of life or property. Generally, things (lives, homes, autos) are *insured*; events are *ensured*; and people are *assured*.

awhile vs. **a while**   *Awhile* is an adverb meaning for a short time. *A while* is a noun meaning a period of time.

bad vs. **badly**   *Bad* is an adjective. *Badly* is an adverb. *I feel bad* is correct if you mean you feel sad, guilty, or in ill health. *I feel badly* is incorrect unless you mean your sense of touch is impaired.

> *That little boy is bad.*
> *That little boy behaved badly.*

beside vs. **besides**   *Beside* means next to. *Besides* means in addition to.

between vs. **among**   *Between* introduces two items; *among* introduces more than two.

bi- vs. **semi-**   *Bi-* means occurring every two. *Semi-* means occurring twice in a period of time.

biannual vs. **biennial**   *Biannual* means twice during the year; semiannual. *Biennial* means every other year.

breath vs. **breadth**   *Breath* means respiration. *Breadth* means width.

can vs. **may**   *Can* refers to ability. *May* refers to possibility or permission.

> *I can attend the meeting if necessary.*
> *She may attend the meeting as long as she keeps*
quiet.

can't hardly   Incorrect. Should be *can hardly.*

canvas vs. **canvass**   *Canvas* is a heavy, coarse fabric. *Canvass* is to solicit votes or opinions.

capital vs. **capitol**   *Capital* means financial assets or the city that is the seat of government. *Capitol* is the actual building in which a legislature meets.

censor vs. **censure**   *Censor* means to ban something considered objectionable (verb) or the person who does such banning (noun). *Censure* means to find fault with.

check up vs. **checkup**   *Check up* is a verb; *checkup* is a noun.

cite vs. **site**   *Cite* means to quote or to call to mind. *Site* means location.

climactic vs. **climatic**   *Climactic* refers to the point of greatest intensity. *Climatic* refers to weather conditions.

complacent vs. **complaisant**   *Complacent* means self-satisfied. *Complaisant* means marked by an inclination to please.

complement vs. **compliment**   *Complement* means to make complete. *Compliment* means to praise.

78

compose vs. **comprise**   *Compose* means to make whole by the combination of parts. *Comprise* means to include.

connote vs. **denote**   *Connote* means to imply or suggest indirectly. *Denote* means to serve as a mark of.

conscious vs. **conscience**   *Conscious* means being aware. *Conscience* means a sense of morality.

continual vs. **continuous**   *Continual* means repeatedly. *Continuous* means without interruption.

council vs. **counsel**   *Council* is a governing body. *Counsel* (noun) is advice or the lawyer or consultant giving it. Counsel (verb) is to give advice.

cover up vs. **coverup**   *Cover up* is a verb; *coverup* is a noun.

credible vs. **creditable**   *Credible* means believable. *Creditable* means worthy of praise or credit.

criterion vs. **criteria**   *Criterion* is singular; *criteria* is plural.

cut back vs. **cutback**   *Cut back* is a verb; *cutback* is a noun.

cut off vs. **cutoff**   *Cut off* is a verb; *cutoff* is a noun.

decent vs. **descent**   *Decent* means appropriate or proper. *Descent* means decline.

defective vs. **deficient**   *Defective* means faulty. *Deficient* means lacking or incomplete in some essential way.

definite vs. **definitive**   Both mean free from ambiguity, but *definitive* refers to something more authoritative and final.

deprecate vs. **depreciate**   *Deprecate* means to play down or make little of. *Depreciate* means to decline in value.

desert vs. **dessert**   *Desert* (noun) is an extremely arid land. *Desert* (verb) means to leave. *Dessert* is the final course of a meal.

device vs. **devise**   *Device* means technique or mechanism. *Devise* means to create.

different from vs. **different than**   Use *different from* unless what follows is a clause.

> *Her culture is different from ours.*
> *Her culture is different than I expected.*

disburse vs. **disperse**   *Disburse* means to pay out. *Disperse* means to scatter.

discreet vs. **discrete**   *Discreet* means tactful or prudent in behavior. *Discrete* means separate, distinct.

disc vs. **disk**   Both mean a thin, flat plate. Use *disk* when referring to computer-related items; use *disc* for everything else.

disinterested vs. **uninterested**   *Disinterested* means impartial. *Uninterested* means indifferent, having no interest.

dive, dived, diving   Past tense is *dived,* not *dove.*

each   *Each,* as a singular noun, takes a singular verb. It can also be used as an adjective.

> *Correct:* Each of the products has its serial number. (*Each* – not *products*, which is the object of a prepositional phrase – is the subject of the sentence. *Each* is singular and therefore takes a singular verb.)

> *Incorrect:* Each of the products have their serial number.

economic vs. **economical**   *Economic* means of or relating to economics. *Economical* means thrifty.

e.g.   Latin abbreviation for *for example.* Avoid; write out *for example* instead. (If *e.g.* is used to introduce an example, however, it should be in italics, followed by a comma.)
either/or, neither/nor   *Either* goes with *or*; *neither* goes with *nor.*

> *Correct:* Neither the radio nor the television is working.
> *Correct:* I knew either the radio or the television was working.
> *Incorrect:* Neither the radio or the television is working.

elicit vs. **illicit**   *Elicit* means to draw out or evoke. *Illicit* means not permitted.

eligible vs. **illegible**   *Eligible* means qualified to participate or be chosen. *Illegible* means unreadable.

eminent vs. **imminent**   *Eminent* means standing out, prominent. *Imminent* means ready to take place, impending.

enormity vs. **enormousness**   The preferred meaning of *enormity* is great wickedness or outrageous crime. *Enormousness* means of tremendous size.
enthused   The use of *enthused* is informal. Use *enthusiastic.*

entitled vs. **titled**   *Entitled* means *having* the right to do or have something. *Titled* means named.

envelop vs. **envelope**   *Envelop* means to surround. *Envelope* means a paper container for a letter.

etc.   Latin abbreviation for *et cetera*, meaning *and so forth* or *and others*. Should not be used with *and* (redundant) or when a list has already been introduced with *for example* or *such as*. Also, use only when it's clear what the next item will be (*Monday, Tuesday, Wednesday, etc. One, two, three, etc.*)

etc. vs. **et al.**   Use *etc.* to mean and other things. Use *et al.* (abbreviation for the Latin *et alii* meaning and others) to mean and other people. Italicize *et al.*

every day v. **everyday**   *Every day* is an adverb. *Everyday* is an adjective.

exceptionable vs. **exceptional**   *Exceptionable* means objectionable. *Exceptional* means rare or better than average.

explicit vs. **implicit**   *Explicit* means expressed directly. *Implicit* means implied.

farther vs. **further**   *Farther* means a longer physical distance. *Further* means to a greater extent.

fewer vs. **less**   *Fewer* is used for items that can be counted. *Less* is used for mass quantities or amounts that cannot be counted. See **amount vs. number.**

> *I cannot complete the project with fewer than six team members.*
> *Our car uses less gas than the competing model.*

first vs. **firstly**   Use *first* instead of *firstly*. The same goes for *second, third,* etc.

fiscal vs. **monetary**   *Fiscal* means of or relating to financial matters (including taxation and public revenues). *Monetary* means of or relating specifically to money.

flaunt vs. **flout**   *Flaunt* means to display showily. *Flout* means to disregard, scorn.

flounder vs. **founder**   Nouns: *Flounder* is a kind of fish. *Founder* is a person who originates something. Verbs: *Flounder* means to struggle ineffectually. *Founder* means to fail or collapse.

follow up vs. **follow-up**   *Follow up* is a verb. *Follow-up* is a noun.

forego vs. **forgo**   *Forego* means to go before. *Forgo* means to abstain from.

formerly vs. **formally**   *Formerly* means previously. *Formally* means according to form or custom.

fortuitous vs. **fortunate**   *Fortuitous* means happening by chance. *Fortunate* means happening favorably.

gamut vs. **gantlet** vs. **gauntlet**   *Gamut* means an entire range or series. *Gantlet* means a literal or figurative flogging. Technically, g*auntlet* means a glove. It is usually used in the phrase *throw down* or *take up the gauntlet* (throw down or take up a challenge).

garnish vs. **garnishee**   *Garnish* means to decorate or adorn. *Garnishee* means to take by legal authority.

gibe vs. **jibe**   *Gibe* means to utter taunting words. *Jibe* is a sailing term that means to shift forcefully from one side to the other. Informally, *jibe* means to be in agreement or harmony with.

good vs. **well**   *Good* is an adjective *(good things)* or a noun *(do good in the community)*. *Well* is generally used as an adverb *(Things are going well.)* or a noun *(in the well)*. *Well* can also be used to mean in good health *(I feel well)*.

> *Correct:* I feel good.
> *Correct:* I feel well.

> *Incorrect:* He performed good.
> *Correct:* He performed well.
> *Correct:* He gave a good performance.

historic vs. **historical**   *Historic* means having great and lasting importance. *Historical* means happening in the past.

i.e.   Latin abbreviation for *that is*. Avoid; write out *that is* instead. (If *i.e.* is used to introduce an explanation, however, it should be in italics, followed by a comma.)

illegal vs. **illicit**   *Illegal* means prohibited by law. *Illicit* means prohibited by law or custom. (Illicit behavior is not necessarily illegal.)

impassable vs. **impassible** vs. **impassive**   *Impassable* means incapable of being passed or crossed. *Impassible* means incapable of feeling. *Impassive* means showing no sign of feeling or emotion.

imply vs. **infer**   *Imply* means to suggest without stating directly. *Infer* means to assume or conclude.

> *She implied in her statement that she had won.*
> *He inferred from her statement that she had won.*

in vs. **into**   Use *in* to indicate location. Use *into* to indicate movement.

84

He stayed in the house.
He went into the house.

indiscreet vs. **indiscrete**   *Indiscreet* means lacking in prudence or tact. *Indiscrete* means unable to be divided into parts.

ingenious vs. **ingenuous**   *Ingenious* means marked by cleverness and originality. *Ingenuous* means showing childlike or innocent simplicity and candor.

in regard to   Not *in regards to.*

inside   Not *inside of.*

irregardless   Not a word; use *regardless* or *irrespective.*

it's vs. **its**   *It's* is a contraction for *it is.* *Its* is a pronoun indicating possession (meaning *belonging to it),* just like *his, hers, yours,* and *ours.* Even the best writers inadvertently swap the two, so every time you use *it's* or *its,* double check your meaning.

It's going to take a long time to photocopy this whole packet.
The copy machine has a mind of its own.

judicial vs. **judicious**   *Judicial* means of or pertaining to the judicial (legal) branch of government. *Judicious* means characterized by sound judgment.

lay vs. **lie**   *Lay* means to place something on a surface. It must be followed by an object. *Lie* means to recline or rest on a surface. It does not take an object.

You can lay your coat on the bed.
You'll feel better after you lie down for a while.

85

led vs. **lead**   *Led* is the past tense of to lead (which means to direct). *Lead* is the present tense of to lead.

less vs. **fewer**   See **fewer vs. less.**

liable vs. **libel**   *Liable* means responsible or likely. *Libel* means a defamatory statement.

lie vs. **lay**   See **lay vs. lie.**

like vs. **as**   *Like* means similar to. It is used with a noun or pronoun that is not followed by a verb. *As* means in the same way or manner. It is used before clauses, which contain verbs.

> *She looks like her mother.*
> *He did as he said he would.*

like vs. **such as**   *Like* introduces an item that is similar to something else. *Such as* introduces an item that is an actual example of that thing.

loath vs. **loathe**   *Loath* is an adjective that means unwilling. *Loathe* is a verb that means to detest.

mantel vs. **mantle**   A *mantel* is a shelf. A *mantle* is a coat or cloak.

may be vs. **maybe**   *May be* is a verb phrase. *Maybe* is an adverb meaning perhaps.

me vs. **myself** vs. **I**   Use *I* as the subject of a sentence; use *me* as an object. (See **pronouns,** Page 42.) Do not use *myself* as a replacement for either *me* or *I*. *Myself* should be used only as a reflexive pronoun – meaning the same person does and receives the action – or as an indication of emphasis.

> *I injured myself when I fell down the stairs (reflexive).*

I myself will deliver the documents (to give emphasis).

moral vs. **morale**   *Moral* means of or relating to the principles of right or wrong. *Morale* means the mental and emotional condition of an individual or group.

naval vs. **navel**   *Naval* means of or relating to a navy. *Navel* means bellybutton or a type of seedless orange.

on vs. **onto**   *On* means supported by or in contact with. It implies a state of rest. *Onto*, in contrast, means movement to a position on. It implies movement up and on.

one of the only   Avoid using this phrase. What you mean is *one of the few.*

only   The position of *only* in a sentence frequently determines the meaning of the entire sentence. Notice the change in the meaning of the sentence when *only* takes various positions, emphasizing different elements of the sentence:

> Only she *told me that she saw him.* (Nobody else told me.)
> *She* only told *me that she saw him.* (She may not have told the truth.)
> *She told* only me *that she saw him.* (She told no one but me.)
> *She told me* only that she saw him. (She didn't tell me anything else.)
> *She told me that* only she *saw him.* (Nobody else saw him.)
> *She told me that she* only saw *him.* (She didn't hear him or talk to him.)
> *She told me that she saw* only him. (She didn't see anyone else.)

87

overdo vs. **overdue**   *Overdo* means to do too much. *Overdue* means late.

passed vs. **past**   *Passed* is the past tense of to pass. *Past* means having occurred in a time before the present.

peak vs. **peek** vs. **pique**   *Peak* means the highest point. *Peek* means to steel a glance at. *Pique* means to arouse a person's feelings, usually in anger or resentment.

percent vs. **percentage**   *Percent* means per hundred and is usually used in place of the % symbol. *Percentage* means a more general portion or part of a whole.

persecute vs. **prosecute**   *Persecute* means to harass or hunt down. *Prosecute* means to bring legal action against.

perspective vs. **prospective**   *Perspective* means angle of vision or point of view. *Prospective* means likely to come about.

personal vs. **personnel**   *Personal* means individual, private. *Personnel* means a group of people employed by an organization.

phenomenon vs. **phenomena**   *Phenomenon* is the singular form of the word meaning either an observable thing or a rare and significant fact or event. *Phenomena* is the plural form.

practicable vs. practical   *Practicable* means feasible or possible. *Practical* refers to something that is both possible and useful.

precede vs. **proceed**   *Precede* means to come before. *Proceed* means to go forward or continue.

premier vs. **premiere**   *Premier* is an adjective meaning first in rank or quality. *Premiere* is a noun meaning a first public performance or exhibition.

prescribe vs. **proscribe**   *Prescribe* means to dictate or lay down as a guide (used in reference to medical prescriptions or therapy). *Proscribe* means to prohibit.

principal vs. **principle**   *Principal* means most important (adjective) or person in a leading position of authority (noun). *Principle* means a basic truth or rule.

prove, proved, proving vs. **proven**   *Prove, proved,* and *proving* are forms of the verb to prove. Use *proven* only as adjective.

pseudo- vs. **quasi-**   *Pseudo-* means false or counterfeit. *Quasi-* means somewhat or partial.

quid pro quo   Latin for *one thing for another*. Usually used in a legal context. Place in italics.

raise vs. **rise**   *Raise* means to elevate or to pick something up. It must be followed by an object. *Rise* means to move from a lower to a higher position. It can also mean to increase in amount or value. It does not take an object.

> *She can raise her head slightly and eat solid food*
now.
> *I am sure she will rise quickly in the company.*

reason, used with *because*   The use of the word *reason* with the word *because* does not make sense. *Reason* already implies causation.

> *Incorrect:* The reason she was fired is because she
> was late all the time.

Correct: The reason she was fired is that she was late all the time.

Correct: She was fired because she was late all the time.

regardless not irregardless

respectfully vs. **respectively**   *Respectfully* means with respect. *Respectively* means individually.

respective vs. **respectively**   *Respective* is an adjective that means pertaining to two or more things separately. *Respectively* is the adverb form of *respective*. It means separately, in the order designated.

seasonable vs. **seasonal**   *Seasonable* means suitable to the season or circumstances. *Seasonal* means varying in occurrence according to the season.

semiannual   Twice a year; same as *biannual*.

set vs. **sit**   *Set* means to put or place somewhere. It is almost always followed by an object. Its past tense is also *set*. *Sit* means to be seated or located. It does not take an object. Its past tense is *sat*.

> *You can set the papers on the chair for now.*
> *Would you like to sit on the sofa or in the chair?*
> *She sat on the board for almost 10 years.*

set up vs. **setup**   *Set up* is a verb. *Setup* is a noun or an adjective.

should vs. **will**   *Should* means ought to and implies a belief. *Will* is a prediction.

some time vs. **sometime** vs. **sometimes**   *Some time* means a period of time. *Sometime* means an unknown or unspecified time. *Sometimes* means occasionally.

> *It will be some time before she arrives.*
> *She will arrive sometime tonight.*
> *She sometimes stops by in the evening.*

stanch vs. **staunch**   *Stanch* means to stop the flow of. *Staunch* means strongly built or steadfast.

stationary vs. **stationery**   *Stationary* means not moving. *Stationery* is a type of writing paper.

suit vs. **suite**   A *suit* is a set of clothes. A *suite* is a group of things, such as software, pieces of furniture, musical movements, or rooms.

take over vs. **takeover**   *Take over* is a verb. *Takeover* is a noun or an adjective.

telecast vs. **televise**   *Telecast* is a noun meaning a TV broadcast. *Televise* is a verb.

than vs. **then**   *Than* means in comparison to. *Then* means at that time or soon afterward.

> *He is a faster typist than I am.*
> *Learn to type correctly, and then concentrate on*
speed.

that vs. **which** vs. **who**   *Which* refers to things, and *who* refers to people. *That* can refer to people or things, but use *that* sparingly when referring to people. Use *who* instead.

In introducing a nonessential clause, *which* should be used only to begin a description that could be deleted without changing the meaning of the sentence.

> *Yesterday's board meeting, which started at 3 p.m., ran for two hours.*

Which started at 3 p.m. is a phrase that is not essential to the sentence's main meaning. *Yesterday's board meeting ran for two hours* makes sense on its own. Nonessential material is usually set off by commas. Therefore, if you would pause at the beginning and end of a phrase when speaking, you probably have a case for *which*.

That is used for essential material. Without essential material, the sentence would change its meaning – or make no sense at all.

> *The company that makes the chips we use filed for bankruptcy.*

Take out *that makes the chips we use* and you're left with, *The company filed for bankruptcy.* What company? And why is it relevant? This is a case for *that*.

their vs. **there** vs. **they're**   *Their* is the possessive form of they (meaning *belonging to them*). *There* means at that place. *They're* is a conjunction meaning they are.

> *I looked over their proposal and was unimpressed.*
> *I put the proposal over there.*
> *They're presenting the proposal tomorrow.*

this vs. **that**   *This* refers to something close by or present. *That* refers to something that has already been pointed out. If two things have already been mentioned, *this* refers to the one that is closer in time or place.

> *I like this one better than that one.*
> *He said she was the best employee. I'm not sure how*
> *I feel about that.*

threw vs. **through**   *Threw* is the past tense of *throw*. *Through* means via or across. *Thru* is not a word.

to vs. **too** vs. **two**   *To* means toward or until. *Too* means also. *Two* means 2.

trade in vs. **trade-in**   *Trade in* is a verb. *Trade-in* is a noun or an adjective.

trade off vs. **trade-off**   *Trade off* is a verb. *Trade-off* is a noun or an adjective.

try and   Incorrect; use *try to*.
undo vs. **undue**   *Undo* means to reverse. *Undue* means inappropriate or excessive.

viz.   Latin abbreviation for *namely*. Avoid; write out *namely*.
wait for vs. **wait on**   Use *wait on* only when referring to hospitality or service *(e.g., waiting on tables)*. Otherwise, use *wait for*.

was vs. were   See **subjunctive** entry in Chapter 2.

well   Do not hyphenate a modifier that includes the word *well* when it comes after the word it modifies. Hyphenate when it precedes the word.

> *Her efforts were well intentioned.*
> *Her well-intentioned efforts were ignored.*

where, used with *at* or as a substitute for *that*   *Where* used with *at* is grammatically incorrect.

> *Incorrect:* Where is the firm's headquarters located at?
>
> *Correct:* Where is the firm's headquarters?

Where as a substitute for *that* is also incorrect.

> *Incorrect:* I saw on television where they arrested the robber.
>
> *Correct:* I saw on television that they arrested the robber.

who vs. **whom**   The distinction between *who* and *whom* is one of the most confusing in all of grammar. Technically, *who* is the subjective form of the pronoun, while *whom* is objective.

When deciding whether to use *who* or *whom,* determine where the action is. If who is doing the action, use *who. (Ellen, who reports to Joan, came to our meeting.)* If the action is being received or if the word is an object of a preposition, use *whom. (I don't know whom I should choose. Joan, to whom Ellen reports, came to our meeting.)*

> *Correct:* Ellen is the person to whom I report.
>
> *Incorrect:* Ellen is the person who I report to.

Some grammarians now accept the use of *who* whenever it comes at the beginning of a sentence. (*Who did you visit?* Instead of *Whom did you visit?)*

whose vs. **who's**   *Whose* means belonging to whom. *Who's* is a contraction meaning who is.

> *Whose desk is that?*
>
> *Who's going to sit at that desk?*

with regard to   Not *with regards to.*

your vs. **you're**   *Your* is the possessive form of you (meaning *belonging to you*). *You're* is a contraction meaning you are.

   Don't lose your briefcase, which you're about to drop.

Top 30 Misspelled Words

(spelled correctly here)

accessible
accommodate
acquaintance
adviser
bankruptcy
calendar
chargeable
committee
conscious
consensus
embarrass
exaggerate
feasible
homemade
indispensable
judgment
liaison
manageable
maneuver
millennium
necessary
omission
privilege
recommend
referral
separate
sizable
suspicious
tendency
toward (not towards)

Top 10 Most Frequently Misused Terms

1. **affect** vs. **effect**   *Affect* (verb) means to influence or change. *Effect* means to bring about (verb) or result (noun).

    > *That movie affected me quite a bit.*
    > *The effect of that movie was powerful.*

2. **among** vs. **between**   *Between* introduces two items; *among* introduces more than two.

    > *I am deciding between a red couch and a blue couch for the lobby.*
    > *I think the tan couch is my favorite among the choices.*

3. **amount** vs. **number**   *Amount* refers to the quantity of something that cannot be counted in individual units (sugar, money). *Number* refers to something that can be counted in individual units (packages of sugar, dollars).

    > *The amount of help we received was unprecedented.*
    > *The number of people who helped was unprecedented.*

4. **bad** vs. **badly**   *Bad* is an adjective. *Badly* is an adverb. *I feel bad* is correct if you mean you feel sad, guilty, or in ill health. *I feel badly* is incorrect unless you mean your sense of touch is impaired.

    > *That little boy is bad.*
    > *That little boy behaved badly.*

97

5. **can** vs. **may**   *Can* refers to ability. *May* refers to possibility or permission.

> *I can attend the meeting if necessary.*
> *She may attend the meeting as long as she keeps quiet.*

6. **farther** vs. **further**   *Farther* means a longer physical distance. *Further* means to a greater extent.

> *The airport was farther away than I expected.*
> *Her explanation of the problem only confused me further.*

7. **fewer** vs. **less**   *Fewer* is used for items that can be counted. *Less* is used for mass quantities or amounts that cannot be counted. See **amount vs. number.**

> *I cannot complete the project with fewer than six team members.*
> *Our car uses less gas than the competing model.*

8. **it's** vs. **its**   *It's* is a contraction for *it is*. *Its* is a pronoun indicating possession (meaning *belonging to it)*, just like *his, her, your,* and *our.*   Even the best writers inadvertently swap the two, so every time you use *it's* or *its,* double check your meaning.

> *It's going to take a long time to photocopy this whole packet.*
> *The copy machine has a mind of its own.*

9. **than** vs. **then**   *Than* means in comparison to. *Then* means at that time or soon afterward.

> *He is a faster typist than I am.*

98

Learn to type correctly, and then concentrate on speed.

10. **whose vs. who's**   *Whose* means belonging to whom. *Who's* is a contraction meaning who is.

> *Whose desk is that?*
> *Who's going to sit at that desk?*

Composing Office Documents

Recommendations for Emails, Memos, and Reports

There are certain guidelines to follow when you write any kind of office document. Other guidelines are specific to the type of document. In this section, I provide some general ideas on composing business documents, as well as some brief, more specific tips on writing emails, memos, reports, and international correspondence.

Some General Guidelines

Know why you're writing. Before you write anything longer than two or three paragraphs, write down the answer to this question: *Why am I writing?* (For example, *To secure funds for the system enhancement, To propose a new approach to employee communications)* Keep this answer in front of you as you write; it's your objective. Include nothing in your document that doesn't relate to or support your objective.

Organize your document. The most basic, and usually the most effective, way to organize any business document is to present the information in descending order of importance.

An exception to this rule occurs when your reader might be reluctant to accept your point of view. In that case, consider presenting information in the opposite order, from least to most important, gradually bolstering your case and ending with your strongest point. The danger with this approach, of course, is that the reader might lose interest and stop reading.

More complex documents sometimes require additional organizing principles. Some other ways to present information include:

❑ Chronological order

❑ Compare-and-contrast format

❑ Problem-solution format

❑ Cause-to-effect format (This approach is good only when you want to explain why something happened or what you think will happen in the future.)

When deciding which format to follow, put yourself in your readers' shoes. Determine how your readers will logically think about the topic, and pick an organizational method that will match their logic. Whatever organizing principle you use, it's still a good idea to follow the most-to-least-important guideline within sections and paragraphs of your document.

Omit details that will be of interest to only some readers in the main text. Instead, include them in appendix section at the end of the document.

Make it easy on the eyes. Aside from using correct spelling and grammar, there are several ways to make your document easy to read:

❑ Use wide margins and ample white space.

❑ Left-justify your text; that is, align your left margin, and keep your right margin "ragged" for ease of reading and a more inviting look.

❑ Indent at least five spaces at the beginning of paragraphs. Another option is to separate paragraphs with line breaks (block style).

❑ Indent lists.

102

❏ Use plenty of headings and subheadings.

❏ Highlight important points with bullets.

❏ Include a table of contents for documents of ten pages or more.

Headings and subheadings guide your readers through your document and show which topics are more important than others. They help readers find information they need so they can scan the rest. Use primary headings for the main sections of the document and subheadings for sections within those sections. Make the headings at different levels graphically distinct. For example:

BOLDFACE SMALL-CAPITAL LETTERS FOR HEADINGS
Boldface Lower-case Letters for Subheadings
Italics for Sub-subheadings

Make the headings as informative as possible. Also make headings at the same level of importance grammatically parallel (for example, all subheads on the same level begin with verbs).

Bullets allow readers to see information at a glance. They are an excellent way to highlight key points, but reserve them for that purpose. Overusing bullets robs them of their impact. There is no set format for bulleting, but here are some guidelines:

❏ Limit each bulleted item to a few lines.

❏ Make bulleted items grammatically parallel.

❏ List only a few bulleted items at a time.

❏ Capitalize the beginning of each bulleted item.

❑ Be consistent in punctuating items, which can end with a period, comma, semicolon, or nothing at all.

Make it easy to understand. Visual techniques are not the only way to make your document accessible to the reader; word choice can help or hinder readers' understanding, as well. Here are some tips for making your document easy to comprehend:

❑ Stay in the same person (first, second, or third) throughout the document. See **point of view,** Page 41.

❑ Don't be afraid to use *I.* First person is common in business documents now. It can keep writing from sounding stilted, making it clearer and more personal. *(I distributed the survey* is clearer and sounds more energetic than the passive, *The survey was distributed.)*

❑ Be consistent with verb tenses within sentences and paragraphs: If you start in the present tense, end in the present tense. If you start in the past tense, end in the past tense – unless there is a logical reason to change tenses.

❑ Minimize brackets, slashes, dashes, and parentheses. Use contractions unless the document is extremely formal.

❑ Don't use words unless you're certain of their meaning. If you are even remotely in doubt, look a word up in the dictionary – or don't use it.

Grab and hold the reader's attention. Use strong openings and closings in any document you write. In particular, the first paragraph should grab the reader's attention – not by being unusual or outrageous, but by presenting most important information clearly and engagingly.

Adopt a conversational tone. Big words and stilted language turn readers off. The simpler and more conversational you can make your writing, the more likely your audience will want to keep reading. Test your writing by reading it aloud to see how it sounds. If it sounds wooden and artificial to you, it will sound that way to your reader.

Use more *you* words than *me* words in all but the most formal documents to show respect and consideration for your reader and to support that conversational tone. When your *you* words *(you, your, yours)* outnumber your *me* words *(I, me, my, mine)*, your readers will more readily accept what you tell them without even knowing why.

By all means, sound adult, but not parental. When you give instructions or make recommendations or suggestions, resist sounding superior or protective. Avoid such words and phrases as *should, never, always, remember to,* and *be* (or *make) sure.* Treat your readers as your intellectual equals.

There are several effective ways to end a document. They include reiterating key points, drawing a conclusion or making a judgment, making recommendations, and suggesting a course of action.

Summarize your ideas. An executive summary at the beginning of a paper is helpful, particularly for longer documents. Like an abstract in a technical paper, an executive summary presents the key ideas of a document in a few sentences or paragraphs (a page at the most). An executive summary allows people who can't read the full text to grasp your main points quickly.

For extremely long documents, consider including brief summaries at the beginning or end of each section.

Proofread, proofread, proofread. Use your spell-check tool, but don't stop there; it won't catch words that are spelled correctly but misused *(to* for *two, at* for *an).* If you have time, print the document and proof it in hard copy, as errors are easier to catch on paper. Consider asking a strong writer to review it and give you feedback.

Emails

Keep messages short. Emails are best suited for quick, day-to-day correspondence. If your message is very important or very long (more than 250 words, or half a printed page) consider sending it as a Word file or making it a memo. Because people receive so many emails daily, a printed document may add weight to what you are saying.

Use informative subject lines. The recipient of your email should be able to get the gist of your message by scanning the subject line. "Today's meeting" is more informative than "Meeting," and "Today's meeting cancelled" is even better.

Give context. Include the original email or some other type of context when replying to a message, even if you respond immediately. Most people get dozens of emails daily, and a simple "Yes" or "No" without context can be confusing.

Be conscious of screen length. Keep your messages short and be conscious of screen length. Have the most important information appear right away, so the reader doesn't have to scroll down to find it.

Break up paragraphs. It's hard enough on the eyes to read from a computer screen without having to slog through a long, dense paragraph. When in doubt, chop things up.

Be professional. Because emails are often conversational in tone, it is tempting to think of them as a different species from other business documents. But while emails may be less formal than other documents, they shouldn't be less professional. Follow the same conventions you would in any other business correspondence:

❑ Write in complete sentences.

❑ Capitalize the beginning of sentences.

❑ Use proper punctuation.

❑ Proofread before sending. If it's a particularly important email, print it and proofread it in hard copy.

Two other tips:

❑ Avoid using all caps. Not only are they equivalent to screaming, but they can also be difficult to read.

❑ Do not use emoticons (smiley faces, etc.). They're fine for personal emails, but not appropriate in most business contexts.

Assume your email will be forwarded. People other than the intended recipient may see your email. Emails are often forwarded, and in some cases, companies can even retrieve deleted messages. A good thought to hold as you write an email is to omit anything you wouldn't want exposed on *60 Minutes.*

Memorandums

A memorandum is an informal report that is usually five pages or fewer in length. Confirm this detail in your company, however; some companies want memos to be only one page long.

Common ways to present information in a memo include:

❏ Inverted pyramid format (most to least important ideas)

❏ Prioritization format (priorities listed in order of importance)

❏ Problem-solution format

❏ Compare-and-contrast format

❏ Chronological order

Two other memo tips:

❏ Use *Subject* or *Re* lines that are as informative as possible.

❏ Alphabetize lists of comparable words, products, or people – especially people – to avoid distracting your readers with "ranking" games.

Reports

A report is longer, more detailed, and often more formal than a memo. Reports should include, at a minimum, the following components:

❏ Table of contents

❏ Executive summary

- Body

- Conclusion

- Appendix

- Bibliography

The format or structure of a report is often prescribed precisely by company rules or convention. Before you begin, confirm your company's format.

If appropriate, include a recommended course of action in the concluding section.

In a report that includes recommendations, it can be quite effective to present the recommendations at the beginning of the document, and then build support for them in the following text. Readers always want to know "Why?" This format leads them to their answers.

Because reports are so dense, they can be difficult to follow. Therefore, it's particularly important to use lots of headings and subheadings in reports, as well as to leave ample margins and space between topics and to number every page.

In writing formal documents, keep your language as clear and straightforward as in more casual documents, with two adjustments:

- Avoid contractions.

- Avoid addressing the reader directly, with conversational references to *you.*

International Correspondence

Be aware of the culture and the relationship. If you are corresponding with someone in another country, your company has probably established a relationship with their company. If possible, meet with an individual in your company who can tell you about the relationship between the two companies and perhaps something about the business culture, as well. Having this background information will help you establish an appropriate relationship with the individual(s) with whom you'll correspond.

Find out how to address the recipient. Because business relationships in other countries are often more formal than in the United States, address your recipient by his or her last name until invited to do otherwise. Even if you are on a first-name basis when you speak, it's best to use last names in written correspondence. Also include in their address any honorary titles or advanced degrees they might hold (*Ph.D.*, etc.). One way to avoid offending colleagues from another country is to follow their lead: Mimic the way they address you.

Choose an appropriate tone. Finding out about the conventions of the other culture will help you choose the appropriate tone. If you're in doubt, err on the side of formality, as informality is sometimes considered rude in other countries. Avoid words that could be considered demanding (such as *must*). Do not attempt to be funny; humor usually does not translate well between cultures and is often considered inappropriate. Be unfailingly courteous and respectful.

Avoid slang, jargon, idioms, figures of speech, and emoticons. When composing a business document that will be read by natives of another country, avoid slang, jargon, idioms, figures of speech, and any other words or phrases that could be misinterpreted or misunderstood. Emoticons are inappropriate in any business correspondence.

Be particularly conscious of spelling. Correct spelling is extremely important in international correspondence: If a word is spelled incorrectly but is still a word, recipients may find an unintended meaning when they look it up in the dictionary.

Consider approaching your topic indirectly. In some cultures, it is considered rude to bring up business right away. Soften your approach with personal greetings or the written equivalent of small talk before addressing the subject at hand. Even when discussing the meat of your document, consider using a more indirect approach than you might normally use. In some cultures, subtlety and reading between the lines are the norm.

Don't assume all cultures are alike. Do your research on the customs of individual countries, even if they are in similar regions or located close to one another.

Keep in mind that date formats differ. Many countries other than the United States express dates as follows: 4 September 1973. Keep this in mind when writing *and reading* numerical forms for dates (9/4/73) so that months and days are not confused. Unless you are filling out forms where the date field is limited to six or eight digits, write out the complete date to avoid any chance of misunderstanding.

Offer alternatives to written correspondence. To establish a comfort level and reduce the opportunity for misunderstanding, suggest a phone call or videoconference to discuss your topic – but only if you and your correspondent can converse in the same language fluently. Follow up any phone calls with written confirmation of their content, especially any decisions that were made.

111

Be mindful of time zone differences. Your contact in another country could be many hours behind or ahead of you, depending on which of the world's 24 time zones he or she lives in. Find out early in your project the time difference between your two locations, and keep this difference in mind when you correspond. (Ask about "time changes," too; other countries have their own versions of Daylight Saving Time, and their changes may take effect on different dates.) If you are using email, don't expect instant responses. Check your contact's time before placing a phone call.

Confirm format before sending attachments. If you email attachments, ask your contact what format to use. If your contact cannot access or read the documents you send (and vice versa), discontinue sending attachments and use a mail service (U.S. Postal Service, FedEx, UPS, etc.).

Remember you are representing your company – not yourself. The impression your contact has of your company may depend almost entirely on his or her impression of you. As sparkling and fun-loving as your personality may be, presenting yourself as a competent, professional businessperson is what matters in this relationship. Represent your company in the way you know your company wants to be represented.

112

Top 10 Tips for Writing Office Documents

1. **Decide early how you will organize your document.** The most common, and often most effective, technique is to present information in descending order of importance.

2. **Make your document easy on the eyes** by using plenty of white space, ample margins, headings and subheadings, and bulleted lists of key information.

3. **Present your key ideas in an executive summary.** This will allow people who can't read the full text to grasp your main points quickly, especially if the document is long.

4. **Use strong openings and closings.** Engage your reader's interest immediately. Methods of concluding a document include reiterating key points, drawing a conclusion or making a judgment, making recommendations, and suggesting a course of action.

5. **Use informative subject lines in memos and emails.** "Today's meeting" is more informative than "Meeting," and "Today's meeting cancelled" is even better.

6. **Keep email messages short.** If your message is very important or very long (more than 250 words, or half a printed page) consider sending it as a Word file or making it a memo. Have the most important information appear in the first screen of the email, so your reader doesn't have to scroll down to find it.

7. **Follow the usual conventions when writing emails:** Use correct spelling, punctuation, and capitalization. Do not use emoticons (smiley faces, etc.). Proofread before sending.

8. **Make documents of five pages or fewer memorandums.** Documents longer than five pages are usually reports. Confirm with someone who knows your company's conventions, however.

9. **Include at least the following parts in a formal report:** table of contents, executive summary, body, conclusion, appendix, and bibliography.

10. **In international correspondence, avoid jargon, idioms, figures of speech, and any other terms that could be misinterpreted or misunderstood.** Consider being more formal and indirect in your writing than you might otherwise be. Research the customs of the individual country. Be unfailingly respectful and professional.

Bibliography

Alred, Gerald J., Charles T. Brusaw, and Walter E. Olin. *The Business Writer's Handbook.* 6th ed. Boston: Bedford/St. Martin's, 2000.

Bell, James K., and Adrian A. Cohn. *Handbook of Grammar, Style, and Usage.* 3rd ed. New York: Macmillan Publishing, 1981.

Blake, Gary, and Robert W. Bly. *The Elements of Business Writing.* New York: Longman Publishers, 1991.

Danziger, Elizabeth. *Get to the Point.* New York: Three Rivers Press, 2001.

Geffner, Andrea B. *Barron's Business English.* 3rd ed. Hauppauge, New York: Barron's Educational Series, 1998.

Goldstein, Norm, ed. *The Associated Press Stylebook and Libel Manual.* New York: The Associated Press, 1999.

Piotrowski, Maryann V. *Effective Business Writing: A Guide for Those Who Write on the Job.* New York: HarperCollins Publishers, 1996.

Ross-Larson, Bruce. *Powerful Paragraphs.* New York: W.W. Norton & Company, Inc., 1999.

Riveting Reports. New York: W.W. Norton & Company, 1999.

Stunning Sentences. New York: W.W. Norton & Company, 1999.

Strunk, William Jr., and E. B. White. *The Elements of Style.* 4th ed. Needham Heights, Massachusetts: Allyn & Bacon, 2000.

About the Author & Editor

Alicia Abell is a Washington, D.C.-based writer and editor. In addition to writing for a wide variety of consumer publications, including *Washingtonian* magazine and *U.S. News & World Report,* she has edited for the Motley Fool, America Online, and Aspatore Books.

Ms. Abell has a BA in English from Dartmouth College and an MA in education from Harvard University.

Jo Alice Hughes has been an editor for Aspatore Books since 2001. She worked for many years in corporate communications at Nationwide in Columbus, Ohio, primarily writing and editing speeches and other documents for the company's C-level executives, managing communication plans for internal customer groups, and editing employee newsletters.

Ms. Hughes has a BS in education from Delta State University in Cleveland, Mississippi, and taught English at the high school level for several years.

ASPATORE

C-Level Business Intelligence™